Praise for
Cut Chaos and Find Balance

"Through imminently relatable personal stories, Rachel Balducci shows us how to see past the chaos to focus on what really matters in life. This book will be a great source of peace to any mom who feels overwhelmed."
—**Jennifer Fulwiler**, SiriusXM radio host and author of *Your Blue Flame*

"In *Overcommitted: Cut Chaos and Find Balance*, Rachel Balducci has written a master playbook for seeking peace and achieving balance in our crazy and over-scheduled world. Rachel shares her own journey through the competing priorities of raising six children, returning to full-time work, all while running the household and attending to the family's growing needs.

Learning the hard way to slow down and reestablish the proper order of things brought Rachel to a place of inner peace while seeking to follow God's will for her life. She generously shares the lessons she learned along the way as well as providing instructions so that you can do the same. This book is aimed right at families who struggle with trying to do it all and is a prayerful resource to becoming more like Mary and less like Martha."
—**Mary Lenaburg**, author of *Be Brave in the Scared: How I Learned to Trust God during the Most Difficult Days of My Life*

"*Overcommitted: Cut Chaos and Find Balance* is a much-needed antidote to the endless expectations of our over-scheduled, hyper-connected, and pressure cooker culture. With humor, authenticity, wisdom, and a whole lot of faith, Rachel offers encouragement as well as concrete tips on how to avoid the pitfalls of overwhelm and burnout.

She reminds us that we aren't only meant to be fruitful, but we were designed to flourish and to lead joyful, meaningful lives where we are no longer slaves to our to-do lists. A must-read for anyone who has ever felt overwhelmed and overworked, *Overcommitted* invites us to make a more conscious effort to notice, appreciate, prioritize, and to ultimately find our peace and purpose in God."

—**Kate Wicker**, author of *Getting Past Perfect: How to Find Joy & Grace in the Messiness of Motherhood* and *Weightless*

OVER
COMMITTED

Cut Chaos and Find Balance

RACHEL BALDUCCI

Published by
The Word Among Us Press
7115 Guilford Drive, Suite 100
Frederick, Maryland 21704

24 23 22 21 20 1 2 3 4 5

ISBN: 978-1-59325-385-1
eISBN: 978-1-59325-386-8

Design by Suzanne Earl

Library of Congress Control Number: 2020902799

Made and printed in the United States of America

CONTENTS

Foreword

I'll never forget the day, years ago, when I raced home from a visit to my parents' house. I had six small kids at the time, and I was racing because we needed to get home in time for my oldest son's basketball tournament. The drive was over an hour long, but I had calculated just enough time for us to stop by the store to buy new basketball sneakers.

If you have small children, you know why I had been putting off this task. You know the drill: park at the store, unbuckle everyone, hold some kids' hands and place some kids in the cart, and then enter the store. Keep multiple children from breaking or stealing anything while helping one child try on and choose a "cool enough" pair of sneakers that cost a small fortune. Wait in line while wrangling children who hang like tiny monkeys from the cart and from your limbs, pay for the sneakers, and then head back to the van where you buckle multiple small bodies into car seats for the ride home.

When we arrived home, I rushed to throw together dinner, and my son ran to his room to change for his game. Moments later, he reappeared and asked, "Where are my new sneakers?"

I caught my breath. I knew immediately where they were. My son's new basketball sneakers were in the shopping cart where I had left them, in the parking lot at the store, over an hour away.

Perhaps I was doing too much. Perhaps you are doing too much too.

We moms are particularly gifted at multitasking and taking on many responsibilities. We take on one thing at a time, and we can put on a pretty good show of keeping all the balls in the air. But sometimes it's too much. We don't even know that we are overextended, burned out, and running on fumes. It's only when life catches up to us, with the drama of forgotten basketball sneakers or some other ball we might drop, that we pause, take a breath, and think to ourselves, "Holy cow, something has got to give."

We all sometimes find ourselves overcommitted, and that's why I am grateful for this book. Because where we struggle sometimes to see where we are doing too much, a good girlfriend can sit us down over a cup of coffee and say, "Hey, you need to stop."

And that's just what Rachel Balducci does in these pages. Like a good girlfriend or a sister who gets it, she sits us down and helps us to see that we need to figure out what our priorities are and let go of some stuff that doesn't matter quite so much.

With honesty and humor, Rachel shares her own struggles and helps us to see we are not alone in the crazy. Without preaching or prescribing, she offers tools we can use to figure out how to balance our many priorities and commitments, how to know when we need to readjust, and how to find peace and joy in the midst of it all. I am grateful that Rachel is just this sort of friend to me in real life, and delighted to see that now she can be just that sort of friend to you in this book.

Read on, overcommitted mom! There is a promise of peace in the pages that lie ahead. The peace that comes not from "doing it all," but from focusing on what matters most.

Danielle Bean
February 27, 2020

CHAPTER ONE

The General Problem of Overcommitment and Burnout

Chances are that you're reading this book because you have a lot going on in your life. With that in mind, I'm going to respect your busy schedule and jump right in. Let's get to it.

What is overcommitment, and how do you overcome it? I want to say, up front, that this isn't a book about doing less. Not necessarily. It's about doing the right things. It's about learning to say no to what you shouldn't be doing so that you can say yes to what you should.

That's the heart of the matter.

We want to say yes to the good, wonderful, and amazing tasks and projects and errands in life and no to all the other stuff.

Now, I can hear you thinking about that and wondering if I'm a little crazy. Because doing the laundry and running carpool and balancing the bank account don't always seem like wonderful tasks. But they have to get done. After all, aren't those items all necessary?

Of course they are! But at the heart of avoiding burnout and overcommitment is learning to do these necessary things that bring balance into your life without running yourself ragged with too much other stuff. A balanced life is part of the foundation of a full and rich life.

But this also isn't a book about a bare-bones existence. It's tempting to think that in order to avoid feeling overwhelmed and tired and worn out, we have to say no to anything other than what has to get done—that in order to avoid burnout, we must learn to say no to every request outside of our basic needs for survival.

That isn't the case.

It's not about always saying *no*, but about learning when and how to say *yes*.

In his book *Essentialism: The Disciplined Pursuit of Less*, author Greg McKeown says that saying yes too much can rob us of a greater good: "Only once you give yourself permission to stop trying to do it all," he writes, "to stop saying yes to everyone, can you make your highest contribution towards the things that really matter."[1]

He gets to the heart of this concept when he asks the following: "Have you ever found yourself majoring in minor activities?"[2]

Oh man, that is a gut punch. And it makes me a little sad.

How many of us, if we are honest with ourselves, would answer yes to that? We run around feeling tired and over-stretched, and we wonder what we have to show for it all? We fly through our day doing ninety to nothing, chipping away at lots of little things that don't seem to add up to something big.

But this isn't a book about quitting your job, running away from home, and following your one true dream, whatever that might be. We are real people here—real people with real lives. We do have hopes and dreams and goals, and these can exist within the sometimes-mundane tasks we have to do.

It's complicated, but we can get it all done.

Before we go any further, I want you to understand this: I'm not offering suggestions about how to glamorize ordinary life, or help find the one thing that's going to feed your soul. Well, I do offer the one thing—but spoiler alert: it's Jesus.

You should find this comforting. Life is filled with opportunities, adventures, hobbies, and projects. But if you don't seek Jesus, none of those other things will fill the hole in your heart that only he can fill.

The Right Stuff

Balance and truth are at the heart of a book about overcommitment and learning how to avoid it. And so this is a book about finding balance in the midst of all we have going on, and learning to seek out the truth about what we should be doing in the first place.

And all of this includes the mundane and the grand. It includes everything we have to do and everything we want to do. It's about learning to find the right activities and knowing when to do all of them. Or some of them. Or perhaps none of them, if we're really off target and need to regroup in order to discover what the right stuff is for us.

Tackling overcommitment isn't simply about doing less. It's about saying yes to the right things and experiencing the peace that comes when you learn to do that. And it's also not about how to bilocate or drive faster or strategically map out your day so you can do twice the things in half the time.

God did not create hurry as your go-to setting in life, and hurry isn't the solution for feeling overwhelmed.

Many of us lead lives that feel overwhelming. For some of us, this only happens occasionally. We have a few days that are "packed" or extra crazy. That's normal. Short stints with lots going on are part of life.

But if we've had these negatives feelings for extended periods of time, then we might have a problem. We can do anything for a short while, but if we're living at an open-ended, rat-race pace, then we have to make a change. Being over-extended is not good for us physically, emotionally, or spiritually.

It's like the change we do with food resets such as Whole30 or a season of fasting. We all have those times, usually after a vacation or the holiday season, when we feel a tad fuller in our gut and know we have to get a grip. We start saying no to sweets during the week, perhaps, or we stop eating in between meals. Maybe we stop buying those amazing cookies that we keep in the freezer—those little mint chocolate wafers that we hide behind the frozen chicken breasts and pull out when no one is around, eating ten or fifteen and only stopping when we feel truly awful.

But I digress.

The point is, we are quick to recognize the importance of boundaries in certain areas of our lives. When our eating is disordered, our body lets us know. When our house needs a cleaning, the rings around the toilets are a good indicator.

But what if we've gotten off track in everyday life too? We feel burned out and unable to find a stopping point. How do we get back to peace and joy when we've said yes to too much? This is especially challenging when we've said yes to good things or to things that seem nonnegotiable. What then? If everything we're doing has to be managed, where do we go from there?

It's much easier to recognize a need to ditch junk. Our calendar and daily schedule are a little harder to assess.

There's a Plan for That

At the heart of overcoming overcommitment is knowing that God has a plan. We have to establish that at the front end of this discussion. God has a plan for your life, including the long haul, and the minutiae of the day-to-day.

Do you believe that? This can be difficult to accept, especially for those of us with a tendency to overcommit. Maybe we know God has a plan, but we're pretty sure it all depends on us. "I and I alone must figure out what it is I'm supposed to do." "I have to determine my responsibilities and then establish a plan for getting them done."

If we operate with that as our starting point, however, we're going to struggle. And believe me, problems arise when you see yourself as the answer to everything going on around you. "If not me, then who?" That can be a good attitude, but only within reason.

We're not going to spend time playing the blame game. It's less important to determine whether we're the problem when it comes to overcommitment (we are. The end.) and more important to focus on the variables that have led us to this point.

Topping the list of these variables is how we see ourselves.

When we try to find our worth in *what we do* instead of *who we are*, we experience burnout. When we say yes to requests because of how it makes us feel, we become overcommitted. If we have arrived at the conclusion that our identity comes

Our worth *doesn't* come from the places we go or the things we accomplish.

from all the moving parts of our day, the amazing things we have going on, and how impressive it all looks, our thinking is disordered and will lead to exhaustion.

We are not what we do. We are not what we don't do. Our worth doesn't come from the places we go or the things we accomplish. Isn't that a relief?

Our talents and gifts and abilities are all from God, and we use them for his glory. But these things (and they really are just things) don't make God love us more, even if they do make us feel better about ourselves.

The most important thing we can do is to keep God in the center of it all—to regularly, every single day, ask God what he wants from us:

"What would you have me do this week, Lord?"

"What about today?"

"Lord, what is your will for me in this very specific time of my life?"

But what if the answer is nothing? That's kind of terrifying.

My mom turned seventy not long ago, and in recent years she has had health struggles. She and my dad have raised eight children and now have almost thirty grandchildren. My mom has been an active, pioneering type of woman who has twice battled and beat breast cancer.

But her health has impacted her activity level, and it's a big shift. Recently, however, she has found great comfort in the midst of this. It's become difficult for her to leave the house, and she can't be left alone either. My dad still teaches at the private school down the street where all eight of us kids went and that my children now attend. He loves his job, and it's an important part of his ability to care for my mom.

Some generous and caring neighbors—friends of my parents for years—have stepped in to help, creating a weekly care schedule. Every weekday, women come in and spend time with my mom, visiting with her and sometimes helping to clean the house.

This has brought great peace to my dad and to me. But it was very difficult for my mom at first. She hated it, as a matter of fact. My mom wanted to be completely independent and she didn't want people around all the time. She didn't like having other people clean her house (cleaning is her thing!). All in all, it was a struggle.

And then, she had this moment of grace. She called one day to tell me about a wonderful visit she had with a friend who had come that day. During the visit, mom had noticed how her willingness to allow these women to come in and serve was good for them as well! My mom realized that what God had her doing, in this season of her life, was being someone willing to be served.

Her willingness is a sign of her tremendous openness to God's plan. It only became easy for my mom when she saw it as a part of what God was doing, not just for her but for everyone involved. It wasn't about weakness or neediness. It was about allowing God to work with her where she was in that moment—an act of love, an act of grace, an act of humble submission to God's plan.

I can relate, to a very small degree.

Years ago, when I was pregnant with our fourth child, I found myself on bed rest. It was a very difficult time. We had our first four babies, all boys, within five years, and being pregnant with my fourth child in such a short amount of time felt a little awkward.

What made matters worse was that I had to rely on others. It's one thing to have a bunch of babies and manage your own life, thankyouverymuch. But to be on bed rest so that the baby wouldn't come too early—that was tough.

For several months, friends made meals for us, picked up and cared for our children (ages one through four) during the day, and came in and cleaned while I just sat there. For a while, it felt humiliating.

And then I leaned in. It was for my own good and, more important, for the good of this baby. I started to embrace the help and feel gratitude instead of shame. I tried to focus less on how I felt my body was failing me, and more on the generosity of all those friends helping me to get through.

That change of attitude helped me so much. In the center of it, I found God instead of failure.

My attitude shift brought great freedom as well. Because in a very small way, I recognized that my worth did not come from anything I did. While I was tempted to feel worthless as I sat around all day and watched others care for my family, I was existing as a child of God.

I still had a lot of learning to do on that front, but it was a small taste of this truth—that our worth cannot be defined by what we do. It was a unique season because I wasn't tempted to overcommit—there was nothing I could commit to do!

Doing Versus Being

When we talk about being overcommitted, that's generally because we are *doing*. We go and do and get it done, and usually we try to get lots done.

The story of Martha and Mary, found in Luke 10:38-42, used to be very painful for me. As someone who likes to get stuff done—especially the nonnegotiable to-dos like the care and feeding of children—I struggled with what I thought that story meant.

Jesus goes to visit his good friends, and while he is there Mary sits at his feet to listen while Martha busies herself with getting things done. They have a dinner guest—Jesus—but Mary sits while Martha works.

For years, I would think of that Scripture passage when I felt a nudge to spend time in prayer. I resented it, to be honest. I felt like my yes to being married and having children voided my ability to spend the time in prayer that I was sure Jesus would prefer. I would sit and try to pray— "at his feet" (Luke 10:39)—and I would hop right back up. If the babies were napping, that's when I could actually turn over a load of laundry quickly or unload the dishwasher without a small child grabbing a knife.

So I had this complicated and pretty negative view of Mary and how we were supposed to somehow be like her but at the same time not allow everything to fall apart. I should somehow sit here, relax, focus on Jesus, and read Scripture while keeping up with every other area of my life at the same time.

And of course, as you probably already know, that isn't the point of the story. Not at all.

The reason Mary has chosen the "better part" (Luke 10:42) is not because she sits around while Martha works. Mary chooses the better part—the best part—because she's *totally* available to Jesus, and not just available as a workhorse.

Mary opens herself up emotionally and spiritually, sitting at the feet of Jesus and waiting on his words. Through that, she disposes herself totally to him. She is peaceful about putting aside her own plans.

Doing is not a bad thing. God needs us to be his hands and feet. The great saints inspire us in this regard. As St. Teresa of Ávila so beautifully tells us, Christ uses us to love his people.

Christ has no body now but yours. No hands, no feet on earth but yours. Yours are the eyes through which he looks compassion on this world. Yours are the feet with which he walks to do good. Yours are the hands through which he blesses all the world. Yours are the hands, yours are the feet, yours are the eyes, you are his body. Christ has no body now on earth but yours.[3]

For this very reason, we must live a life that seeks God in everything. When we do that, every part of our day is an act of love for Jesus. When we do that, we can experience God's presence in the midst of all we do. We make ourselves totally available to God and to saying yes to him. And we are open to hearing whatever it is he would say to us.

So the issue of overcommitment is equal parts spiritual and practical. It's being in tune with the Father and the Son and the Holy Spirit, and it's also being a human in a human body. We do have commitments and people to care for. It's a tricky balance.

So we've established that seeking God's will in all things is key. Once we do that, we can look at the life God has given each of us.

Recognize this however: overcommitment isn't about the unique details of your life. It isn't because you have too many kids or a husband who works a lot or because you work a lot. It's not because your parents are struggling with their health or because you come from a family that likes to do a lot together. These details can contribute to feeling that you're overwhelmed, but they're not the root cause. The root cause is how we let it all add up to be too much.

That's good news! I don't want anyone out there thinking they're destined to be overcommitted or always feel overwhelmed because of where they landed as a human. You can have control in your scheduling and your doing and your committing to things. Life circumstances do not make you a victim of overcommitment.

I had an interesting conversation in this regard one day when I was getting my teeth cleaned. That, of course, means the conversation was really me listening to my hygienist after I asked her how she handled her personal schedule and all she had going on.

"I'm working on a book about being overcommitted," I said in between scraping. "Would you mind telling me a little bit about how you manage your day?" Her reply fascinated me.

The woman has one son--and I don't say "just" one son because when I listened to her describe a typical day and a typical week, I knew that her one son and one husband and one life with all it had going on in it was every bit as full and brimming as my life with my six children and one husband and one life.

Her week consisted of many of the same activities as mine. She ran errands and met up with friends. She had a house project she was in the middle of and a menu to plan. She made time for exercise and bringing her child where he needed to go. Her life had a lot of moving parts.

She had the life God had given her with the circumstances therein. Same with me. Same with you.

This isn't the Pain Olympics, where we compare who is the busiest and most exhausted. That's always a temptation. It's not about looking around and assessing that your life is the hardest because you always have the most going on.

Years ago when my children were tiny, Paul and I invited a group of college guys to have dinner with us once a week. One night, after a very long and exhausting day with small boys keen on escaping my watchful eye, the guys came over to eat.

"How was your day?" I asked one student, and he replied by putting his head back and inhaling deeply and going into all the ways life was so very overwhelming right now.

Of course I wanted to roll (roll so very hard) my eyes into the back of my head. Yeah, I wanted to say, your life is *so hard*, taking care of yourself and trying to find time to study.

But that was mean-spirited of me. The truth is, we all have our lives. That's it. We are called to live the life God has given us, and we can either sit around and talk about how much harder our own path is or we can rejoice in what we've got going on and find a way to enjoy it.

In reality, when I was single and a college student, my life also felt plenty full. And I felt stressed at times. And now that I'm a college professor, I see how stressed those students feel. My job isn't to stand there and tell them how easy their lives are, because they're not. Some days it might look pretty easy to me from my vantage of trying to juggle family life and a job, but what college kids go through is a big deal. My job for these students is to encourage them in their quest to manage everything they have going on, in the same way I'm working on that as well.

As for my dental hygienist, I sat and listened. She described all her family had going on—practical events and fun events, personal projects and activities they did as a family. And it was the stuff of life. It's what we all work to manage. We juggle helping kids with homework and getting them places, keeping the house clean and taking care of the bodies God has given us. We spend time with family and neighbors and generally run around doing activity after activity.

It's called being alive, and it's wonderful!

But when the collective total of a day or a week gives us chest pains or a spinning brain or finds us in the fetal position on the couch wanting to fake a coma (oh, you've never been there? Aren't you lucky!), that's when we know it's time for change.

And the change, obviously, can't be getting rid of things like children, a husband, homework, or helping out a friend. You can't quit calling your mother or your sister.

But what it must mean—what it absolutely, unequivocally, and without a doubt has to entail—is learning to set boundaries and make a plan. It must mean finding time throughout the day and the week to catch our breath.

That's how we tackle being overcommitted. We learn to say no to things, and we learn to prioritize. But we also learn that the abundant life is full and wonderful. And there will always be appointments on our calendars and places to go. We will always have a to-do list and stuff to buy and some closet somewhere in the house that needs to be organized.

That's good; it's a sign we're alive!

Priorities, Self-Care, and the Great Adventure of Life

Let's consider our priorities. We have to understand what those are so that we can determine where we can cut the fat. Certain aspects of life can't be on the table for axing. Right off the bat, for example, I know that whatever else I have going on, my priorities are the following:

- Time with God
- Caring for my husband
- Caring for my children
- Taking care of my household

Those are my four nonnegotiables.

The most challenging, for me, is caring for my husband. It's not that I don't adore him. He's my very favorite person in the world to spend time with. But for some reason, he's also the easiest to "call right back" or cancel on or even plan to tell something important to and totally forget because we get interrupted. Spouses can get dangerously overlooked, and while that sounds dramatic, I really mean it. If we don't fight to make time for our mate, we can look up to discover we've totally lost touch.

While we should be aware of how our children are doing and we should make efforts to spend quality time with them, children are much harder to overlook than our spouse.

And this is where I get back to the challenge of being overcommitted in the first place. The reality is that if I'm not taking care of myself, I can't take care of anyone else. If my relationship with Paul feels strained because *I'm* feeling strained, then I'm not necessarily able to pay him all kinds of attention. When I feel personally burned out to the core, I have nothing left to give. If my response to my family's needs is that I simply can't handle one more request (we've all been there!), then it's time to start looking at my commitments and figuring out what has to give.

God first, then family, and everything else after that. That's a well-ordered life.

When we manage those variables and put them in proper order within our lives, we can tackle the beast of overcommitment and emotional fatigue.

But it's going to be okay. It's going to be great! You can acquire the tools that will help you decide what you're supposed to be doing with your time. You can learn how to avoid becoming overcommitted in the first place.

Let's get started.

THREE TIPS

1. God has a plan for you and for your life.
2. He knew what he was doing when he gave you your spouse and children, your family and friends.
3. God wants our lives to be full and joyous, but we don't need to take on so much that we feel sad or exhausted.

PERSONAL REFLECTION

1. Do I currently feel like my life is out of control?
2. Of all that I have going on right now, what three areas are causing me the most stress?
3. Is there anything within these areas that I can tweak, minimize, or streamline to make my life feel more peaceful?

MOMENT OF GRACE

Prayer Tip

The thought of spending daily time in prayer can feel overwhelming, especially if you are in a time in your life when every waking minute is occupied with caring for others. A good first step is generally asking God to show you when you could take time to be with him. You will be amazed at the time that appears and the moments that you become aware of once you make this request.

Don't overshoot your headlights with prayer. Instead of setting a goal that is unrealistic (a daily Holy Hour, for instance), find a few minutes of quiet in your day—time that God really will provide for you if you ask him to show you—and learn to spend time with Jesus. Ask him to reveal his great love for you.

Prayer Starter

Father,
I abandon myself into your hands;
do with me what you will.
Whatever you may do, I thank you:
I am ready for all, I accept all.

Let only your will be done in me,
and in all your creatures—
I wish no more than this, O Lord.

Into your hands I commend my soul:
I offer it to you with all the love of my heart,
for I love you, Lord, and so need to give myself,
to surrender myself into your hands without reserve,
and with boundless confidence,
for you are my Father.

—Charles de Foucauld[4]

CHAPTER TWO

It All Starts with Prayer

When I returned to full-time work outside the home, it was a big decision. I had spent twenty years doing freelance writing and speaking at conferences, a mostly home-based approach to work that had served us well in the season of little children and a husband busy with his law practice.

I was ready for change, but I was scared. Only a few years earlier, I had abruptly quit work that I was doing outside the home because I was burned out. When Isabel, our youngest child, started kindergarten at the same school that our other children attended, I volunteered to teach a class there. Eventually this commitment led to teaching four classes, and by the time I stopped, my volunteer work had become a part-time job that involved a lot more than I had signed up for. I quit halfway through the school year and felt terrible about it.

Even though the job had been part-time, it had been consuming, and my life seemed to be spinning out of control. All my yeses felt like way too much.

I learned something valuable in that season, however: you can't make decisions simply to please other people. I was guilty of that—I didn't want to disappoint anyone by admitting that I simply could not do what I had volunteered to do.

Sometimes we try to please people without any pressure from them whatsoever. So, the only person who can free me up to make my own decisions is me. I have to be free to do what is best. That calculation looks different for everyone. Sometimes we stay because we made the commitment or because we need the money. Sometimes we go because we need money and it isn't available where we currently work.

The point is this: when you know something isn't right, you feel it.

But what was difficult for me—what it took me a while to grasp—was that even though I was teaching at my kids' school and even though it was an amazing place filled with amazing people, that didn't automatically make it the right place for me.

I was shocked when I realized this. When the dust had settled, I finally understood: God had me there for a season, but when the season was over, he had different plans for me.

When I tried to ignore what he was telling me and I kept pushing through, trying to stay where I was, the fruit in my life was not good.

I was confused because the school was such a gift and was staffed by generous people who keep Jesus as the center of the whole endeavor. I figured that if we were giving children an awesome education and also talking a lot about Jesus—then where else in the world would God want me to be?

The problem was that I never stopped to consider the answer to that question. I also wasn't open to hearing alternatives. It is possible that something can be really excellent and involve the best people doing the best work, and it is still not where you're supposed to be.

When I finally realized that, it was mind-blowing to me.

This experience was crucial in forming my understanding of God's plans and how we come to know his plans for us. I was selling Jesus short. I was so focused on wanting the school to be amazing that I didn't stop to think that Jesus could do it without me. He could handle it—really, he could.

So fast-forward a few years. I had quit the job and worked through my embarrassment over feeling burned out and my shame over leaving halfway through the year. I had made peace with my decision. When a new job opportunity arose, I was pretty scared to go for it.

"What if I crash and burn again? What if people think I'm horrible for quitting that one job a few years ago and not going back when I felt ready to work again? What if . . . ?"

The bottom line was that I had to ignore all the doubts and fears but also make sure it wasn't actually prudence and wisdom giving me pause. Sometimes our concerns are valid, but sometimes we have to push through. This is when prayer and seeking the advice of wise people are so important.

As I started to work through whether I could say yes to this new endeavor, my spiritual director encouraged me, saying, "If you are 100 percent available to Jesus, he can walk you through."

So that's what I began to focus on—giving Jesus my plans and being willing to hear him say no or giving Jesus my plans and being willing to hear him say yes.

You've Got a Friend

Sometimes God has things in store for us that are different from what we imagined. It can take tremendous trust, as well as wisdom and God's grace, to get through to his plan in the midst of challenging circumstances.

We get this grace and wisdom and trust by seeking friendship with Jesus. We cultivate that friendship by getting in the habit of offering everything to him, and then being willing to let him do as he will.

That's scary, isn't it? That level of trust takes real relationship. And that relationship only comes from making the time for prayer and showing up and practicing the presence of God.

I have found that the more time I spend in prayer—the habit of daily quiet time with the Lord—the more prayer becomes a time of peace and joy. The answers I'm seeking reveal themselves to me throughout my day, and decisions regarding what to do feel more like a natural extension of my thought life. I'm not spinning my wheels trying to come up with solutions. The answers seem to peacefully present themselves.

And so, a conversation about feeling overcommitted and burned out is, at its core, a conversation about prayer and the ways in which prayer is the remedy, ort antidote, to feeling overwhelmed.

If you are at a place in life where time in prayer seems out of the question, then simply ask God to show you how you can spend time with him.

"Lord, help me want to pray." That was my very first step toward transformative prayer. I was starting to sense that prayer wasn't something to be marked off a to-do list, but something that I wanted. Not only did I want it—I needed it. Prayer is about relationship, and praying was helping me enter into that relationship with God.

Even if you find yourself unmotivated to pray and thinking it's just another thing you have to do to feel like a decent person, let me assure you: if you pray, you will draw nearer to the Lord, and he will help you figure things out.

Your Call, Your Gifts

God speaks to us in the silence of prayer. He doesn't just help us discover what we need to do, but he helps us find our truest self—the person he created us to be.

Why is this concept so important in the context of feeling overcommitted? Because knowing who you really are helps you to zero in on your gifts and calling, and that helps you have the confidence to say yes to the things you need to say yes to and no to all the other things.

Pope St. John Paul II addresses this longing that each one of us has—to know who we are and God's plan for us. If we turn our gaze to him, we'll find the answer to what our soul seeks:

It is Jesus that you seek when you dream of happiness; He is waiting for you when nothing else you find satisfies you; He is the beauty to which you are so attracted; it is He who provoked you with that thirst for fullness that will not let you settle for compromise; it is He who urges you to shed the masks of a false life; it is He who reads in your heart your most genuine choices, the choices that others try to stifle.

It is Jesus who stirs in you the desire to do something great with your lives, the will to follow an ideal, the refusal to allow yourselves to be ground down by mediocrity, the courage to commit yourselves humbly and patiently to improving yourselves and society, making the world more human and more fraternal.[5]

Jesus is the answer. If you want to change the world, know who you are in Jesus.

I love that the Holy Father speaks of what we have to offer. We will improve society! We will do great things! God takes our humble yes and uses it to build his Church and feed his people and somehow, in some small way, he uses our brokenness and our yes to do great things.

When we talk about gifts and calling, we're focusing on practical skills and abilities that we use to draw others closer to God that at the same time energize us. Beyond the practicalities of our current circumstances, these are talents, or aptitudes, that make life fun. It's stuff we're good at that we love to do!

How do we know what these abilities are? How can we get in touch with these gifts?

As always, prayer is a big part of the equation. And with prayer comes discernment.

In *Discernment: Reading the Signs of Daily Life,* Henri Nouwen touches on what that is: "Discernment is faithful living and listening to God's love and direction so that we can fulfill our individual calling and shared mission," he writes.[6] "Living a spiritually mature life requires listening to God's voice within and among us . . . To discern means first of all to listen to God, to pay attention to God's active presence, and to obey God's prompting, direction, leadings, and guidance."[7]

We spend time in prayer in a way that draws us into a sense of God's leadings. When we become attuned to the gentle push or nudge or leading, we go where God would have us go.

Practically, this can look something like this: You are presented an opportunity, and even though it wasn't your idea necessarily, you find peace in saying yes. You give the opportunity a try, and you find joy within it. And in saying yes to this and in experiencing that joy, you also help others draw closer to Christ.

Here's an example: Our friend J.J. is a husband and father of nine children, two of whom have Down syndrome. J.J. and his wife, Jen, homeschool, and he is also in the diaconate program for our diocese.

One Sunday at Mass, to our amazement, J.J. was the cantor. We had no idea he had any musical abilities, but when he sang the responsorial psalm, there was something beautiful and blessed about his understated style. He sounded wonderful, but not in a way that drew attention to his own abilities.

He had some kind of charism—a special ability—for this task.

After Mass, several of us commented on how moved we were by his singing. He said that a few weeks before, he had the slightest inkling of a thought about being a cantor. He said it was a little strange because he had never sung or performed before—ever.

And then, a few days later, the parish music director asked J.J. if he would consider being a cantor.

Just like that. J.J.'s simple habit of spending time in prayer opened him up in a very gentle way to this service. Even though he was nervous, he trusted in God's gentle nudge.

"The Holy Spirit opened me to the idea," J.J. said, "so I felt I needed to step out of my comfort zone in a leap of faith."

It's possible to draw up an elaborate chart of how and when and why to try new skills. How and when we know what we want to do can be really overwhelming.

Ultimately, it's about having discernment, which comes from spending time in prayer—prayer is the answer again! It's also knowing that we have skills and abilities God has given us—stuff we like to do—and God really does want us to use those gifts! Writing, speaking, painting, hospitality, singing—these are all gifts from God and an important part of our created selves. God wants us to use these gifts because in using them, we draw closer to him.

The best part is how God really will afford us opportunities to use these gifts in a way that fits in with our lives, instead of competing against it. God gave you the life you have, and he gave you special gifts. It all comes from God, and if we trust in his plan, he will gently show us how it can all work together. Maybe not all of it in every single season of our lives, but there will be time to use our abilities in ways that feed our souls and bless those around us.

But we also need to trust in God's timing. If you are a young mama with a lot of small children, this might not be the season to start a public speaking ministry, especially if you are motivated by what you see other women doing. We have to be at peace with our own life circumstances, and even if we know we have gifts in a particular areas, it's important to wait on God's perfect timing.

When we are motivated by comparison or fear (more on this later), it's easy to make dumb decisions.

Peace comes from knowing you are on God's radar and that he has a special plan for you.

Years ago, when I started wanting to get closer to Jesus, I became easily discouraged. I was quick to compare myself to others—to all the amazing people who were doing seemingly amazing things. I went even deeper and considered the greater spiritual bounty of people—I was sure they were much more profoundly spiritual than I was.

The climax of all this self-doubt and discouragement came one day when I made it to the Adoration chapel (a feat in itself in that season) to spend time in prayer. I sat there and started to feel a closeness to Jesus that encouraged and excited me. I began feeling like maybe it was all going to be okay.

A few minutes later, two women walked in. They were friends of mine and wonderful people. So wonderful, in fact, that I was acutely aware of just how wonderful each of them was. And I started to focus, not on Jesus's great love for me, but on his great love for them. They were doing so well in life— even their hair never seemed out of place. I felt so defeated.

There is a way that we can focus on the goodness of others and on their successes and victories and walk away inspired and encouraged. This was not one of those moments. I think Satan was taking something good—my ability to see superstar tendencies in others—and turning it into a threat. I figured those women were killing it in life, and the relationship each had with Jesus was equally booming.

From there I decided that if they were doing so great in life and in personal holiness, then that somehow meant I had to be a step below them. They were great; I was not.

It's embarrassing to remember all this, but that's where I was. I was still trying to find my identity in *doing*, and I was hoping that somehow my activity level would wash holiness

It's *not* self-centered to focus on you and Jesus. It's where you'll find your *deepest identity.*

over into the core of my being. The more I *did*, the better I would feel inside.

I brought this experience to my spiritual director at the time, a holy man named Dan who told me one of the most profound, life-changing, and freeing things I have ever heard: "What Jesus is doing in you, Rachel, he cannot do in anyone else. What he wants to do in you, he cannot do in anyone else."

What a relief; what a joyous discovery!

I don't need to keep up with anyone else. God doesn't want that, and I shouldn't worry about that. I can be happy for other people without focusing on what I think they have going on. I can focus instead on Jesus.

I struggled with this concept for a while—of not worrying what God was doing with those around me. I loved the freedom of the idea, but I had to get used to living it out. Focusing on my relationship with Jesus felt a little self-centered. There are so many people in this world, and I know I'm not the center of it.

But in the words of St. Augustine, "God loves each of us as if there were only one of us."[7]

It's not self-centered to focus on you and Jesus. It's where you'll find your deepest identity. The more you focus on his incredible love for you, the more you'll find who you really are. Further, when you operate out of that love, you'll make decisions based on your true identity, not on a fear of missing out or, even worse, of someone else getting ahead of you.

You can move through your day and your life in spectacular freedom, untethered and ready to do what God would have you do.

When you live in that freedom, you will also be doing your part to help others find new or deeper life in God. As Bishop Robert Barron has said,

We are sent by the Lord to spread his word and do his work. The Gospel is just not something that we are meant to cling to for our own benefit; it is seed that we are meant to give away.

Prayer is not incidental to ministry. It is not decorative. It is the lifeblood of the Church's efforts. Without it, nothing will succeed; without it, no ministers will come forward. At all times pray, pray, pray.[8]

THREE TIPS

1. We can only find our true identity in Christ.
2. In order to have true friendship with Jesus, we have to spend time in prayer.
3. Spending time in prayer is where we experience God's great love for us. This strengthens our identity, which comes from him—a perfect circle.

PERSONAL REFLECTION

1. Do I spend time in prayer? If not, what is blocking me from making time? If it's the circumstances of my life, please show me, Lord, when I can pray!
2. When I spend time in prayer, do I experience God's love for me? If not, have I asked him to show me his love?

3. What is God saying to me? Do I have some sense of what he wants me to be doing?

MOMENT OF GRACE

Prayer Tip

Now that you are aware of how to find time for prayer (by asking God to show you the time!), here's the next transformative step. Instead of showing up for prayer with a list of all the things you need God to fix, focus on God's love for you. I know it might feel weird at first, maybe even selfish, but learning to receive God's love will transform you. There is also plenty of time for intercession in prayer, but at the heart of a real life-changing experience is building your relationship with Jesus.

Prayer Starter

Courage, then, O soul most beautiful, you know now that your Beloved, Whom you desire, dwells hidden within your breast; strive, therefore, to be truly hidden with Him, and then you shall embrace Him, and be conscious of His presence with loving affection. Consider also that He bids you, by the mouth of Isaiah, to come to His secret hiding-place, saying, "Go, . . . enter into your chambers, shut your doors upon you"; that is, all your faculties, so that no created thing shall enter: "be hid a little for a moment,"[9] that is, for the moment of this mortal life; for if now during this life which is short, you will "with all watchfulness keep your heart,"[10] as the wise man says, God will most assuredly give you, as He has promised by the prophet Isaiah, "hidden treasures and mysteries of secrets."[11] The substance of these secrets is God Himself, for He is the substance of the faith, and the object of it, and the faith is the secret and the mystery. And when that which the faith conceals shall be revealed and made manifest, that is the perfection of God, as St. Paul says, "When that which is perfect is come,"[12] then shall be revealed to the soul the substance and mysteries of these secrets.

—*St. John of the Cross*[13]

CHAPTER THREE

An Ordered Day

How many of us have ever wished we had more hours in a day so we could get more done? Other times we count the hours until the day is over. Both of those yearnings can signify burnout. But how are we to manage our time?

Establishing a well-ordered day is a practical challenge, but beginning the day with prayer can make all the difference. Now, I'm one of those people who has found prayer first thing in the morning almost impossible. No matter what time I set my alarm, the minute I get out of bed, I seem to inspire other household members to wake up as well. (Sound familiar?) If I try to get up early, sneak into the front room, light a candle, and sit quietly, someone always seems to come out of nowhere and want to sit with me.

There's nothing wrong with that. It's really sweet. But it seems to defeat the purpose of getting up extra early to spend alone time with Jesus. And yet so often we hear that prayer should be the first thing we do every day.

Here's the solution, shared with me by people with far more wisdom and experience than I. It's not (necessarily) about getting up out of bed and collecting your pile of books and heading to your special spot. If that works for you, that's wonderful! I'm not jealous one bit.

But if that's not where you're at, you can still start your day with prayer. And it can become the first thing you do each day. When you wake up in the morning, in those moments before you are fully awake, get in the habit of opening your mind and heart to Jesus. I once heard this described as those moments before the devil knows you're awake. It's a precious time between you and the Lord. These first few magical moments can set the tone for your day.

If you are in the habit of rolling over and grabbing your phone, I highly recommend you stop doing that. Extensive research demonstrates that there are health benefits related to leaving your phone out of your bedroom routine. I can confirm this, personally. When I get in the habit of looking at a bunch of social media first thing in the morning while in bed or last thing at night before I turn out the light, the fruit in my life is not good.

So don't do that.

Here you are, starting to wake up, perhaps because you hear a baby stirring or because you hear small children scampering toward you. Or quite possibly you have made it to that season when you wake up on your own, without someone's foot poking you in the nose.

Either way, in those moments, as your brain starts to wake up but you aren't moving yet, give your day to the Lord. Thank him for his love for you, and offer every part of your day to him. Ask him, "What are your plans for me today, Lord? Guide my path and bring me peace." And he will.

A few years ago, in an especially hectic season, my spiritual director suggested that I ask God to show me three things he wanted me to do that day. Basically, I started asking God to handle my to-do list—every day. It seemed a little silly, but as with so many other things, I learned that God cares about it. Instead of trying to figure it out all on my own, I gave it to God and asked him to guide me.

God is not going to grab a pencil and write out ideas for you on your notepad. But if you get in the habit of offering your day to him, he will guide you. The more you get in the habit of personal, quiet, and simple meditation, the more peace you'll find as you plan your day.

All in a Day

What is a day supposed to look like anyway? When we speak of a well-ordered day, what does that mean?

One weekday morning a while back, I sat at the bank waiting to see an account specialist. I had no other pressing errands aside from a quick drop-off to the seamstress around the corner, and we had to stay out of the house anyway while some work was being done there. It felt absolutely weird to sit and wait and not feel completely rushed and stressed because things were taking so long. I realized that I rarely live at this pace, and that's not necessarily a good thing.

Life is busy; there's no denying that. But we don't need to think that every open space on our calendar is automatically fair game for filling. If you're feeling frenzied, maybe start budgeting forty-five minutes for the errand you once allotted twenty minutes to.

But a plan is good, whatever that means for each of us. Sometimes the plan means that we commit to accomplishing one thing in particular. Maybe it means that because of all the stuff going on in our family or at work, all we can determine is that most of what has to happen will happen . . . eventually.

If we don't have a plan for our day, the minutiae will kill us. We can say yes to a thousand little things that rob us of our bigger yes. Maybe that bigger yes would have been something that we didn't think we had time for—and something we have now lost because we spent our days running around crazed.

These kinds of conversations can get tricky because one person's understanding of planning is what another might call OCD (obsessive-compulsive disorder). Strategic calendar planning only works if you find a system that your brain and temperament can handle.

Imagine that you have a pile of rocks, pebbles, sediment, and sand. And you want all of this to fit inside a jar. If you try to fill the jar with the tiny items first and then add the bigger ones, you won't have much luck. But if you put the big items in first, everything will settle in and fit. First go the rocks, then the pebbles, and then the sand and sediment can filter in around them.

In short, things fall into place when we put our tasks in the right order. In fact, they fit perfectly. But if we give priority to the small things, we won't have the time and energy for the more critical items that we should have taken care of first. The result? We feel overcommitted, not because we are wasting time, but because we have given the wrong things too much importance.

I mentioned earlier that I used to start and end my day on my phone. I was using the precious first moments of my day and blessed last moments to look at social media—pictures of other people doing cool stuff, looking fabulous, and traveling to interesting places.

I was giving top priority to something that should have been a side note or a quick check at some point during the day. I was treating social media like a big rock when in fact it was a teaspoon of sand. When I'm doing first things first, checking Instagram isn't a big deal. But when I treat checking Instagram like a job, that's a problem.

Relaxing has its place, but when it comes to using your phone, be honest with yourself. Most phones have limits you can set so you don't spend too much time scrolling. You can also set limits for when you can access certain apps. I finally decided to let my phone allow me to check social media for thirty minutes a day, and only during a certain time of the day. Sounds like a jail sentence? It was, just a bit. But I had allowed my phone use to dominate me, and I needed to take extreme measures to get back on track.

When we talk about priorities and the big stuff—those giant rocks that we need to address first—what does that mean for you? Identifying those will help you facilitate an ordered day. After you ask Jesus what plans he has for you today, in those early-morning moments between sleep and wake, then think through your priorities.

For me, I think about what has to happen. Caring for my children, a plan for dinner, knowing where various family members are going to be, a quick tidying of the house, and going to work. Those are all nonnegotiables.

Once I've thought through my daily schedule, including where I have to be and when, I think about what else we have going on. Is there a meeting that night? Do the kids have sports? Have I fit in time for exercise? If there are no medical appointments or other commitments, do I need to run any errands? Some days running errands is a nice treat, but sometimes I use free time to go home early and rest.

It's a lot to consider, but it's worth considering if I want to have a sense of peace.

Oh, and one last thing. Always have a plan for prayer. In fact, it shouldn't be one of the first things you think about in the morning but one of the last things thought about the night before. Before you fall asleep, decide when you will spend time in prayer the following day. Prayer can quickly and easily fall off your radar and the results are dangerous.

I meet with my spiritual director once a month. Once, when it was time to set up that meeting, I realized I didn't have anything much to discuss. Things were going really well, in fact. The big boys were all doing well and life was moving along pretty smoothly. I was struggling with a little bit of anxiety, and out of the blue, one area of insecurity I had experienced real victory in was creeping back. But just a tad.

I almost canceled our meeting because life felt pretty good. I decided to go, just to pop in really quickly and say hi.

"Things are great," I explained to Bev. "I mean, the only thing besides a bit of anxiety about rejection and insecurity is that I'm not really having a prayer time. But that's just a small thing."

Or course, the minute I said it out loud, I was able to connect the dots. Actually, Bev did that for me. The "no big deal" of not having a prayer time was directly related to the negativity and anxiety—all areas that through prayer and grace God had healed several years before. Why were they back, I wondered, while also not noticing that daily prayer was off my radar?

Here's what was really scary and interesting about this experience. I told Bev that no prayer time didn't feel like a big deal because things in my life, in general, felt pretty good. We weren't in crisis with any of the kids, and the sailing all felt smooth.

You know who loves that? The devil. In fact, when things feel rocky, we are more inclined to run to the feet of Jesus. But when we slowly drift away from being in God's presence and putting him in the center of our day, the devil is all for it. And instead of drawing attention to that, we get a false sense of peace.

I realized, after talking with Bev, that what I actually felt was fuzzy and a little sad. I was focusing on the externals—kids doing alright, Paul and I trucking along, life feeling decent—and I was numbed to the reality. The source of my anxiety and sadness was a lack of prayer.

That very day I got back into time in prayer, and with it came clarity and joy and peace. Thank you, Jesus!

Frenzied Thinking

What if feeling overcommitted is simply a state of mind? I realized one day, in the midst of my perfectly curated daily schedule, that I felt hurried all the time. In an effort to be fruitful and organized, I was going, going, going.

My day would start with an early rise followed by a workout. Then I focused on home life: getting kids ready for school, packing lunches, and tidying up the house. Then I'd head over to work and stop by the Adoration chapel that was next to campus. I always thought of this opportunity as a great way to start my day, and I had arranged my schedule so that I had those twenty minutes in the chapel for quiet contemplation.

Except that I wasn't really starting my day at all. I was already several hours into my day, which isn't a problem unless you want to feel calm and composed when you arrive for Adoration. I rarely did. When my twenty minutes were up, I'd head to campus where I'd gear up mentally for class and get ready to lecture.

Sometimes, in an effort to manage a variety of things, we can get so hyperorganized that life feels like one big rat race. And because I'm a creature of habit and quick to form habits, even fun things like getting my daily caffeine fix became just one more thing to do. I had a plan for exactly where and when that transaction would take place. One giant unsweetened iced tea? *Check!*

One day, I realized that as organized as I was, I still felt exhausted all the time—not physically, but mentally. This was partially the result of starting a new job and working full-time outside the home for the first time in a long time. But another part of it was my attitude, my state of mind. In order to arrive early and feel calm at work, I raced out the door in the morning so fast that my head spun.

Here's what was tripping me up in my turbo-speed hyperorganized daily pace: I was treating all of the items of the day with equal importance and kind of killing myself in the process. Prayer and home life and work life and extra stuff—it's all good. But it needs to have its place, in the right time of the day.

So, I tried something new. I slowed down. I started a reverse method with my to-do list, just for kicks. Instead of racing to get all. the. things. done right off the bat, I took a long view of the day. I set my priorities, but I was okay with those things not happening first. Just because my priorities were the "big rocks" of my day, that didn't mean they had to happen first in the day. It just meant I had to have a plan for when they would happen.

The fruit was transformative. The fruit was peace. The fruit was going back to prayer being the center of the day, and asking God to prioritize everything else. Instead of everything being equally yoked, it was 1. prayer and 2. everything else after that. And because I've invited Jesus to be in the center of it, I have had real peace knowing that I'm doing what I need to do. Things get done just as cohesively, but in a way that doesn't leave me out of breath.

In Difficult Seasons

What about when life is just tough? Intense? How do you manage when you feel overcommitted but there isn't anything you can eliminate from your schedule?

This is a grin-and-bear-it, white-knuckle kind of a time. You know it's going to be challenging for a while, but you find ways to ease the pain.

Having a newborn is a good example of this kind of season. It's a beautiful time, but it's difficult. Or caring for an aging parent. Or managing a household after the departure of a spouse.

I remember the weeks after we had our son Henry. Actually, that's a lie. I should say I *almost* remember the weeks after we had him. Henry is our fifth child, boy number five, born five-and-a-half years after our fourth child. I thought it would be a breeze. Compared to the prior season of baby after baby (and adding babies to the mix of toddlers), I was sure that having one baby with a bunch of older boys would be a snap.

It was not. It ended up being the most difficult pregnancy, delivery, and postpartum experience of them all. Not to freak you out! If you're thinking maybe you should have one more baby after a nice little break, don't let me discourage you. Because here's the thing: twelve years later, I can honestly say, "I survived that!" It was intense and difficult, and I very nearly drowned almost every day.

At the time, my friend Mollie was also pregnant and due to give birth a few weeks after me. Years later, she told me that she saw me somewhere at that time, and I looked terrible. I had what appeared to be gigantic duffle bags under my eyes, I was absolutely sleep deprived, and I'm guessing my hair was a tad rumpled too. I looked so exhausted that it terrified her, because she was about to go through the same thing that rendered me this beat up. And there was no escaping.

We laugh about it now, but in those weeks, it was difficult.

So how do you get through feeling overwhelmed when there is nothing you can do about it? Here are three suggestions:

1. Lower your expectations. That's generally the key to getting through these times. If there is something in your daily and weekly routine that takes up energy you no

longer have, either stop doing it or make it way easier. I have a friend who is working on her PhD. She told me that right now, she has less time for exercise and personal care. It's not ideal, but it's her reality for the moment.

2. Streamline. Make easy meals. Maybe put some toys in the attic so that there isn't as much to clean up every day. Take the top sheet off the kids' beds so that making beds is easier. I'm just saying: think outside the box. You will be amazed at the little ways you can make life a bit easier when you are desperate. Hire someone to clean your house. Don't send Christmas cards that year. It's all gonna be okay.

3. Be kind to yourself. Don't hold yourself to the same standards of order and organization and getting to events that you would if you were in "ordinary time." It really is a season, and you will make it through.

An ordered life does open us up to more yeses, but we must be sure those are the yeses God wants for us.

Some Thoughts about a Calendar

Let's get super practical for a minute about keeping track of your plan for the day and week. You might be someone who works best with large chunks of time open for various activities. Perhaps you do better with having a general plan for every hour. (If that thought made you break into a cold sweat, you are definitely better suited to the "bigger chunks" approach.)

Either way, an actual calendar will make it possible to keep track of everything. It can be paper, or it can be on your phone. As long as you have a way of keeping track of everything you have going on, you'll be able to avoid hyperventilating.

Find a method that works for you. My own approach to keeping track of my day (and week, month, and year) involves a calendar as well as a notebook.

First, I have a yearly calendar that I keep in my kitchen. It's leather bound in book form. I put a lot of thought into this book each year, and I text back and forth with my sister-in-law—she is as calendar oriented as I am—as we get closer to deciding what book we each will use that year.

I pay attention to the layout of the page, the size of the book, and whether or not it stays open (or doesn't) on the week I'm in. I consider if there's enough space to write down what we have going on. I don't want anything too busy. I personally don't need a feature that helps me keep track of water intake, for instance. Less is more, but the right amount of less.

What I do need is a full-week view, along with space to break my day into morning, afternoon, and evening. When my children were little, I organized the day as starting, nap time, and after nap time/afternoon. In those days we didn't have much of an "evening" because children went to bed at 7:00 p.m., and Paul and I only had a few activities to track after that.

As our kids got older, we started having a very active evening life. Now, there are multiple activities going on throughout the day and the evening, and what works best for me is a calendar that allows me to see all those items clearly.

I don't use different markers for different kids—that's too overwhelming for me. It's enough for me to know I'm involved in this activity—either reminding the child he has it or getting him to it. A color-coded system seems like overkill for me.

So there's that calendar. That's the one that keeps track of our coming and going.

Second, I keep a notebook with me at all times. This has my daily to-do list and a running shopping list. I include things I need to get done that day, but not for the week, although items can be bumped from day to day. So the weekly calendar shows meetings, practices, and appointments, and the notebook primarily shows errands I need to run that don't have a specific timeline.

Keeping track of all these moving parts takes some of the frenzy out of my life. Based on my own experience, I recommend establishing a calendar and writing as much or as little as works for you. And then make sure these calendars and lists work for you and don't create their own internal pressure against you.

One last thing: figure out what you can outsource if you need to. Have you heard of grocery home delivery? I have! Ahem. And it changed my life. It actually costs less than going to the store (the annual fee was very reasonable) because I only get what's on the list. In the season we are in, this has brought incredible freedom and peace.

For several year, I hired a college student to vacuum, mop, and clean the bathrooms. It didn't cost very much and saved me two hours a week that I used to go have fun with my kids.

There is a time and a place for everything, and God really wants to lead you to the tools you need to get the job done.

THREE TIPS

1. Ask God to show you his plan for your day. In the early morning moments, before anyone else is up or before you are fully awake, ask God to be with you in all you will do today.
2. Have a plan for the day, practically speaking. What do you have going on? Do you have the margins you need in your day to peacefully do what you have to do?
3. If it's an especially crazy day (or season), streamline life to bring peace. On really busy days, have a plan for dinner that doesn't involve lots of cooking at the last minute.

PERSONAL REFLECTION

1. When I plan my day or week, do I put the right tasks in the right order?
2. If my day is disordered, what do I need to adjust?
3. Do I find myself feeling worn down from the practical parts of my day? What can I do to make this better?

MOMENT OF GRACE

Prayer Tip

Since a lot of this chapter focuses on fast-paced living, let's talk about finding time for family prayer. That can be overwhelming when there is a lot going on. You might not all get home at the same time each evening in a way that affords peace-filled family prayers.

One nonnegotiable I have found with kids and prayers is doing something right when we get in the car. It's simple and quick but also powerful. We buckle up and pray for the day, and sometimes each child offers petitions, sometimes not. And we say one Hail Mary and one St. Michael the Archangel—a prayer for grace and a prayer for protection.

Prayer Starter

Litany of Trust

From the belief that I have to earn Your love
Deliver me, Jesus.
From the fear that I am unlovable
Deliver me, Jesus.
From the false security that I have what it takes
Deliver me, Jesus.
From the fear that trusting You will leave me more destitute
Deliver me, Jesus.
From all suspicion of Your words and promises
Deliver me, Jesus.
From the rebellion against childlike dependency on You
Deliver me, Jesus.
From refusals and reluctances in accepting Your will
Deliver me, Jesus.
From anxiety about the future
Deliver me, Jesus.
From resentment or excessive preoccupation with the past

Deliver me, Jesus.
From restless self-seeking in the present moment
Deliver me, Jesus.
From disbelief in Your love and presence
Deliver me, Jesus.
From the fear of being asked to give more than I have
Deliver me, Jesus.
From the belief that my life has no meaning or worth
Deliver me, Jesus.
From the fear of what love demands
Deliver me, Jesus.
From discouragement
Deliver me, Jesus.

That You are continually holding me, sustaining me, loving me
Jesus, I trust in You.
That Your love goes deeper than my sins and failings and transforms me
Jesus, I trust in You.
That not knowing what tomorrow brings is an invitation to lean on You
Jesus, I trust in You.
That You are with me in my suffering
Jesus, I trust in You.
That my suffering, united to Your own, will bear fruit in this life and the next
Jesus, I trust in You.
That You will not leave me orphan, that You are present in Your Church
Jesus, I trust in You.

That Your plan is better than anything else
Jesus, I trust in You.
That You always hear me and in Your goodness always respond to me
Jesus, I trust in You.
That You give me the grace to accept forgiveness and to forgive others
Jesus, I trust in You.
That You give me all the strength I need for what is asked
Jesus, I trust in You.
That my life is a gift
Jesus, I trust in You.
That You will teach me to trust You
Jesus, I trust in You.
That You are my Lord and my God
Jesus, I trust in You.
That I am Your beloved one
Jesus, I trust in You.

—Sr. Faustina Maria Pia, SV (Sisters of Life)[14]

CHAPTER FOUR

My Vocation, My Time, My Responsibilities

We tend to think of a vocation as something only a priest or member of a religious order has. The rest of us—those who end up remaining single or getting married—are just single or married people.

But we all have a vocation—a unique call from God through which we grow in our relationship with him and our service to others. We each have a mission, and through our vocation, we help to transform the world.

When you think about marriage as a vocation, as opposed to simply finding and committing yourself to your soul mate, it feels a little different. I don't want to take the romance out of your marital situation, but I do want to remind you that there is a lot more to your marriage than falling in love and making a vow to stay together for the rest of your lives.

Whether you are single, widowed, married, or in the religious life, you have a vocation. One of the nice things about embracing the concept of vocation is how compelling that reality can be on those days when you just aren't feeling it. It's possible you will have a few days here and there, or possibly a few weeks or even months when marriage and family life feel like a challenge or when being single feels like a cross to bear—when your state in life doesn't feel like where you want to be, not exactly.

This is when the idea of vocation is very helpful.

When we embrace our vocation, we can move through the day confident that we are moving within God's plan for us. We experience peace and joy, trusting that we're not simply slogging through our activities, but are participating in something bigger than ourselves.

It makes the humdrum of everyday life seem pretty grand indeed!

When I was in college, I spent several summers working with the Missionaries of Charity, the order of religious sisters founded by Mother Teresa. One summer I even met Mother Teresa when she traveled to New York City to receive an award from the Knights of Columbus. The group of volunteers I was with was made up of college men and women who had all gone to the same small private high school—friends from back home who had traveled together for this mission trip.

The guys stayed at a brownstone in the Bronx that had a shelter for homeless men on one floor, the sisters on another floor, and an upper floor for summer camp volunteers. Over in Harlem, the women had a similar setup. Halfway through the summer, Mother Teresa came to receive her award. Somehow—the details are still a little hazy—I ended up sitting next to her at Mass in the tiny chapel in one of the convents.

As you can imagine, those weeks stirred up my desire to be a nun and to do something amazing for God. I was at a critical point in life—halfway through college and about to transfer to a bigger school in a bigger city to focus on my college major.

I was also kinda sorta dating a guy—Paul—who had just graduated from law school. He was ready to move toward marriage and even made a comment during that summer about wanting to buy a station wagon. That freaked me out. Also, I was a few years behind him in age and in my education efforts, and on top of all this, I was now romantically drawn to the idea of being a nun.

When you volunteer with the Missionaries of Charity, you spend a lot of time in prayer. That was good because I needed prayer as I tried to decide between being a nun or investing more time in getting to know Paul. Most of all, I wanted the Lord to know that even though I really liked Paul, I was willing to give him my all if that's what he wanted.

By the end of the summer, it was clear to me that God didn't want me to be a nun. Paul proclaimed his love for me one afternoon, but my decision about the religious life was independent from that. And that was a good thing. I did find myself slightly disappointed that God didn't seem to need me in his special army of "truly holy people" when it turned out that the call to the convent was clearly not there. I offered myself to him, and he didn't go for it.

On the other hand, my feelings for Paul cleared up. I was in love, and God didn't need me to be a nun, so it all worked out.

The big flaw in my thinking, however, was that I saw myself as junior varsity in the holiness department. Because I was going to pursue dating and marriage rather than the religious life, I figured being a saint was no longer a life goal.

Fast-forward a few years. At the end of our summer with the Missionaries of Charity, Paul took a job in Mexico City to work in international law. I moved to Atlanta, got my undergraduate degree, and we carried on a nice, not-too-compli-cated long-distance courtship. We knew we wanted to get married, and that's exactly what we did several months after my college graduation.

It wasn't until a few years later that this concept of voca-tion and what it means *for me* as a wife and mother hit home. Up until then, I saw marriage as something special, but I still considered my experience of offering myself to God for the convent as separate from—and higher than—offering myself to God in general.

As Paul and I got a few years into our marriage, however, I saw that God did in fact want me for himself and that he would draw me closer to himself through my vocation as a wife. I was not a religious sister, but I still had a vocation. God still wanted my yes, and he could even use it to his glory.

I began to see that marriage is a path to sanctification just as any vocation is. Paul and I were building the Church in a different but equally beautiful way just as someone with a call to the priesthood or religious life.

My marriage wasn't about being in love versus not being a nun. It was about doing whatever God asked of *me* and trusting that I was doing what God needed from me in that moment, and in that day.

This understanding came at a convenient time. I had started having babies—all those baby boys that we had so close in age—but I was beginning to see that I was living out my call from God and that I would find holiness here. My nearly-drowning-but-not-quite moment was tied into a growing sense of vocation. The simple yeses throughout my day in that sea-son—yes to wiping this runny nose, yes to changing this dirty diaper, yes to juggling all these tiny humans with my frequent feelings of life passing me by—this was how I was growing closer to God and maybe becoming a saint.

I didn't always feel great fervor, but in my lowest moments, my sense of vocation was a nice reminder that life wasn't passing me by. What I was doing in this moment was exactly what God was asking me to do. It was a relief.

This is the reality of vocation for each one of us. If you are married, through your vocation you can change the world. If you are single, that's how God is using you. A mom? An empty nester learning to adjust? These are all places we might find ourselves, and God can use them all as we live out our vocation.

Considering our vocation within the context of managing our commitments is an important part of how we make decisions. All that talk about vocations and holiness is part of understanding that the work each one of us does *is* part of God's plan. Knowing and remembering that God is using your life to build his kingdom establishes a sense of purpose.

What we are doing with our time and energy is part of God's plan for each one of us. For me, my vocation—my call to be married and be a mother and run a household—is a tremendous part of how I decide what is worth my time and energy.

Each one of us has a vocation. We establish what it is and what the vocation requires depending on our season of life. The mother of young children will require different levels of energy and different needs within the home than the mother of teens. Both require time and energy and attention and love—but in different ways.

Similarly, singles and priests and nuns and empty nesters and widowers will each have their own unique set of life circumstances and commitments.

Boundaries

Ultimately, our focus should not be on whose life is easier or whose life is holier. It's about being aware of our vocation, our primary commitments, and going from there. It's also about establishing boundaries.

One evening, I was talking with my good friend Fr. John. He's been a priest for over thirty-five years, and I've often wondered how men like him manage to run a parish with all of the spiritual and practical matters involved in the job. He told me that becoming a priest should include getting a Master of Business Administration because you become a spiritual father who also runs a small business.

But the answer to doing it all, he told me, was having boundaries. He sets time limits on meetings and sticks to them. He does a good job of using his day off to actually relax. When we had this conversation, we were sitting at the beach, one of Fr. John's favorite places. He has managed the busy life of being a parish priest by knowing his limits and also knowing the importance of R & R—rest and relaxation.

Fr. John's vocation is to the priesthood, but he doesn't have to kill himself in the process of serving others. He's generous with his time and he gets a lot done, but he's at peace in the midst of it.

Our friend Fr. Tim, who was the best man in our wedding a few days before he left for seminary, still makes time to hang out with us whenever he comes to town. He knows that time with friends feeds his soul. On the other hand, we knew a wonderful parish priest who made it clear that he didn't go to parishioners' homes for dinner. That was his boundary. He was friendly and available and a workhorse at the parish level. But he didn't do things like go to dinner.

If priests can have the freedom to set boundaries that help them find peace within their vocation, each one of us can do that as well. We do what we are called to do within our vocation, and we find order and joy in doing that in a way that works for us.

Practically speaking, when you understand what your vocation is, you have a good starting point for determining what really matters. And if you know what really matters, you're on your way to avoiding overcommitment. If your vocation is to marriage and family life, then that will be your priority. That means anything else you're asked to do will need to fit within the framework of your vocation—caring for your family and home life.

In my case, this means that when I review the different parts of my day—the activities I have to do and the committees and meetings I'm choosing to attend—I need to consider how these impact my husband, my children, and the rhythm of our home.

Here's an example. At the private school my children attend, there is a special Mass in the gym on the first Friday of each month. We all look forward to it, even though it requires being out the door by 6:50 a.m.

In order to peacefully make this work, I have to consider a lot of moving parts the night before. I need to know where school uniforms and shoes are. I need to make sure the children have packed their lunches. I need to sign homework notebooks and ask one more time if everyone's homework is complete.

My primary vocation in this scenario is not getting our family to Mass, even though being there is very good. It's making sure that the duties of home life are peacefully covered. Those don't have to be mutually exclusive—I can do both. But in order to manage both Mass and home life, I have to think several steps in advance.

There are similar considerations with other activities. If I want to commit to serving on a committee at school or participating in a Bible study, it shouldn't come at the cost of peace in the home. It's not that I need to say no to everything besides laundry and homework, but I do need to make sure I can peacefully manage getting those things done within my other commitments.

This also doesn't mean my job as a mom is to always put everyone else's needs first. For example, if my middle school son forgets his homework even though I've reminded him a few times, the consequence should be his, not mine. A large part of parenting is teaching responsibility. But I will tell you from personal experience that when lots of things seem to be falling apart with multiple children, it might be time to scale back, if only for a season.

In this equation, I don't set a hard bottom-line number limiting the things I'll do. But I do look at my calendar, think about all the moving parts, and make sure that in general my yeses fit within the responsibilities that come with my vocation.

This goes back to that concept of boundaries. It's knowing—or learning along the way—what you can say yes to and what is too much. It's learning, perhaps, that you can commit to something on a weekday morning, but weekends are generally out of the question. Perhaps it's learning that a weekly commitment is too much, but every other week works for you.

Common sense plays a role here. One of my life dreams is to hike the Appalachian Trail, or at least a small part of it. I know that right now, where I am in life, I'm not a good candidate for heading into the woods, alone, for three to six months. That seems like an extreme example, but when you use that same logic on a smaller scale, it will help you move about your day with order and freedom.

I'm not trying to kill your dreams! Because here's the other great thing—you get to decide what all of this means for *you* and your family. When our boys were little and my husband was working long hours at his law practice, I recognized that I was experiencing burnout. I was home all day with four little boys, and then I had to endure the stressful witching hour (that time before dinner) by myself. I struggled with the reality of Paul's work situation, and I spent a lot of time comparing his daily schedule to the one my father had when I was growing up. My dad was the headmaster of the school I attended, and he came home with us at three o'clock every afternoon.

Of course, my dad had meetings in the evening, but I grew up thinking that all dads everywhere came home after school just like their kids did. It really rocked my world when I realized this was not the case.

I realized, as an adult, that my dad's schedule was a teacher's schedule, but I still spent time noticing all the other working dads in the neighborhood and what time they got home. Paul was usually later than all of them.

I finally arrived at a place of peace when I decided that my job was not to compare myself to everyone else, but to find a plan that brought me peace in our situation. In order to save my sanity, I put two of my boys in preschool. My oldest son was five, and he and his three-year-old brother started going to preschool a few days a week. It was life changing.

Now I had the energy I needed to manage baths and dinner and bedtime by myself (if needed) with a little more grace. I wasn't so burned out from an open-ended day of just me and the four boys from dawn till dusk. I love my children, but I needed the day to have a bit more ebb and flow.

My point in this story is not to convince you to send your babies to preschool. That might not work for you. But I had to make this decision, with Paul, based on what worked best for me. Truth be told—at that point none of my friends were doing it, and it felt selfish and indulgent.

For me, though, it was a lifesaver. It got me through a tough time, and it serves me today as an example of knowing my boundaries and my vocation and making it all fit together.

We have to be free to say yes and no—and commit or not commit—in a way that brings us freedom and supports our vocation. It's about knowing ourselves.

Within your vocation, you are still you. This means that the way you go about your day will look unique for you. Whether single or married, you have a schedule and limits and capabilities that are not identical to every other single or married person you know. You get to figure it out.

Know yourself. Understand your vocation. Be okay with your limits. And don't compare.

The Missionaries of Charity have a convent in Atlanta. Because of some shared connections, and because I had worked with them several summers, I drove them around the city when they were trying to find a location for their ministry. I loaded four sisters into my tiny Honda Accord hatchback and set off, driving to various parts of Atlanta as they got a feel for what they needed.

They finally found the property that worked for them—a house and cottage in a nice part of town. They turned the large home at the front of the lot into a house for women with AIDS and the cottage behind it into the chapel and convent.

Many years later, I was able to return to this place with my children. We visited for a week and volunteered at the summer camp the sisters run for Burmese refugee children. We also went to Mass and evening prayers with the sisters in their chapel. Here's what struck me about being with them as they searched for a house so many years earlier and coming back to see their plans realized: the sisters know what they are doing.

They have a firm sense of purpose, and they make their plans accordingly. The sisters have a very clear understanding of how to run a house for women with AIDS and who is able to stay. They don't take women who need the care of a hospital, for example. They recognize their limits as caregivers, but also trust in God's mercy and grace.

Ultimately, the sisters move through their day in peace and joy because they recognize everything they do as part of God's plan for them within the context of their vocation.

Their day doesn't belong to them; it belongs to God, and he gives it into their care.

Jesus is at the heart of our vocations. He uses our vocations to lead us to his Sacred Heart. As married people, singles, or those called to something other than the religious life, we have the same opportunities to find Christ in the ordinary and extraordinary moments of our days.

We use the circumstances of our vocations—the places we go, the things we do, and the people we encounter—to draw us closer to Jesus. It isn't just quiet time in prayer that leads us to him, although in all we do, we can invite Jesus to be with us. God wants to meet us where we are, and that means in the circumstances of our duties and vocation.

THREE TIPS

1. You have a sacred call in your life—your vocation—into which all your other commitments fall.
2. God will draw you closer to him through your vocation and through all the activities and encounters that your vocation affords.
3. You don't work against your vocation in the midst of your commitments. You work with it.

PERSONAL REFLECTION

1. Do I believe that God has a sacred call for me in my life? Do I trust that the activities of my day and the people I encounter are a part of God's plan for me?

2. Do I consider my primary vocation when I think about what I will say yes to? And what I say no to?

3. Do I accept the limits of my current state in life? How can I find a plan that brings me peace in my current situation?

MOMENT OF GRACE

Prayer Tip

This is actually a tip of what *not* to do. When I first discovered the transformative power of contemplation, I wanted to share it with everyone. I especially wanted my children to learn this a lot sooner than I had. So one night, for family prayers, I told Paul that I had a plan. I pushed the furniture out of the way and created a little altar at the front of the family room. I put several candles there and set out pillows for the boys to kneel or sit on.

Then I lit the candles and told the boys—five of them ages ten and under—that we would sit in absolute silence for fifteen minutes. Five boys, fifteen minutes, and multiple flames.

Four minutes later I was asking Paul through tears why that had been such a disaster. He helped me do the math (boys plus fire equals fiasco) and I realized that just because something was working well for me personally didn't mean I could expect the same results with my entire family. Also, I am a pyromaniac and have given birth to a few of these as well. Prayer time shouldn't have a lot of flames.

After that evening, we went back to the family prayer that works for us—intercession and petition. We go around the room and say what we are praying for. And then we say an Our Father, Hail Mary, and Glory Be. It is beautiful and peaceful and free of flames.

Prayer Starter

Lord, you know how much we need you. Draw us closer to you. Give us peace for each season of our lives. Fill us with your grace and peace, and remind us to trust in you. You love each one of us as if there were only one of us. Order our days so that we can hear your voice and do your will. Let us spread your love everywhere we go, and fill us with a peace that is contagious. Amen.

CHAPTER FIVE

Fear, Worry, and Too Much Yes

A neighbor heard that I was giving a talk on prayer and showed up at my door one day with a copy of Henry Nouwen's book *With Open Hands*.[15] It contained one of the most transformative essays about prayer that I've ever read.

The title alone is the perfect explanation for how prayer should work. It's not about style or using the right books or always covering every base; prayer is about our relationship with our Creator. Do we enter into that relationship ready to tell God all the things he needs to do for us or all the stuff he needs to fix? Or do we enter with open hands, ready to offer ourselves to God, in all our brokenness, prepared to see what he will give us in exchange?

With Open Hands starts with the story of an elderly woman who arrives at a psychiatric hospital "wild, swinging at everything in sight, and frightening everyone."[16] The doctors have to take away her personal items, but she refuses to let go of a small coin in her hand. She clenches her fist, holding tightly to the tiny item. Finally, two people manage to wrench open her hand, struggling with her over a coin that means so much to the her but, in reality, is worth nothing. "It was as though she would lose her very self along with the coin," Nouwen said. "If they deprived her of that last possession, she would have nothing more and be nothing more. That was her fear."[17]

We are, of course, all like that old woman. We hold on to so many things that are worth nothing. We hold on to grudges and anger, to opinions and to past hurts. And we hold on to images of ourselves—perhaps the way we want to be seen or an identity that is wrapped up in what we do instead of who we are.

In order to really let God in and have his way with us, we have to be willing to open our clenched fists. We have to say to God, "I offer it all to you, and I hold nothing back."

We learn to do this a little more every day as we slowly deepen our relationship with God based on trust. "Jesus, I trust in you," we tell him. When we begin to believe, in our core, that Jesus loves us, knows us, and has our best interests at heart, then we can learn to open our hands.

Fear—A Motivator to Nowhere

What are we so afraid of anyway? Go ahead and ask yourself: What am I afraid of?

- Are you afraid that if you say no, it won't get done?
- Are you afraid that if you say no, someone else will get the glory?
- Are you afraid that if you say no, you will miss out on an important opportunity?

Whatever your fear, there is a God-centered solution. If you simply cannot say yes to a request but you are afraid that it won't get done, or if you want to say yes primarily because you want the recognition, or if you're afraid that if you say no you'll never again have such a wonderful opportunity, then it's time to turn to God. It's time to trust that Jesus will take care of everything.

I can tell you right now that the times I have said yes out of fear—out of fear of missing out or of being passed over—the situation has lacked peace and joy. When I miss the mark in my motivators—when I act from fear—the result is havoc and stress, and it's time to reset. Emotionally. Physically.

At one point, I was saying yes to requests because I was trying to be part of something that I didn't need to be part of. I wanted to stay plugged in with a particular group so I took on work that I knew from the beginning was more than I could handle. But I was feeling rejected and I was afraid of being left out, so I said yes to an additional task—I practically asked to be given the task—and it pushed me over the edge.

It was a terrible time, and it came about because of absolutely dreadful decision making on my part. Most of us, at least occasionally, make decisions out of fear or worry—I know I'm not alone. It's exhausting.

I said no once.

Ha! But seriously, I was so proud of myself the day I was able to tell someone no—that I couldn't do what they asked me to do. It was a nice request—I had been invited to speak at a retreat—but as much as I wanted to accept, I knew I didn't have the time.

Sometimes saying no is a matter of switching gears. Here's what I mean. When I first started receiving invitations to speak at retreats and conferences, I treated each request as if piped in on a direct line from the Holy Spirit. If I was somehow on the organizers' radar, I reasoned, God must want me at their event.

There seemed to be some truth to this, at least during that time. I had the time and energy, and my home life was pretty calm, relatively speaking. We didn't have a lot going on outside of normal day-to-day life. If I had to be out of town, I could make a schedule that included who went to play with which friend after school on the days I was gone, and also what dish to microwave for dinner.

It was simple. But as time went on and as I took on other responsibilities and, most important, as my kids got older, it wasn't as easy. Here and there I could swing it, but leaving to speak at a retreat every few weeks started taking its toll. And so, I said no. And it took guts.

It was such a change to switch gears from seeing each opportunity as ordained by God and requiring my assent, to seeing the opportunities instead as something I needed to fully consider. You might be wondering what all this has to do with making decisions from a place of fear and worry. Well, here are the sorts of questions that I was grappling with: What if people forget who I am? What if, by saying no, the requests dry up? Even with these questions, though, I had learned and was continuing to learn to trust that when the time was right, I could start saying yes again.

It's tough to have those fears and worries—to find the courage to let them go and to choose to believe that things will work out. Accepting that it would be okay wasn't the same as being assured that no matter what, the requests would still be there when I was ready to say yes again (though they very well could have been). But I made a decision that was based on trust and the good of my family, and not on the very real anxiety that hovered in the background. The fruit of that decision was greater peace for me and my family in that season.

Trapped or Trusting

Okay, by now you know that Paul and I had our first four children in five years. I know I keep bringing it up, but it was a school of life for me, and I continue to draw lessons from those crazy years.

Our lives, for a short while, went something like this: give birth to a baby boy. Boy turns one. Discover you are pregnant. Nine months later, give birth to a baby boy. Repeat two more times. That was my life. Four boys ages five and under. It made me angry when people told me that I had my hands full. I didn't want to be the kind of person on the receiving end of comments like that. But people apparently felt compelled to say it.

Now that those boys are all in college and I look at mamas with babies and toddlers, I can see why people said that to me. I did have my hands full. My heart was full too. That's what my mom, with eight children, would always say to people who commented about her hands being full: "My heart is full too." As a teenager, I rolled my eyes when she said it, but then I grew up, became a mom, moved past those early frenzied years, and now I get it. My hands were totally full and so was my heart.

Nevertheless, there I was with all my little boy babies and toddlers, feeling very much trapped at home, not only physically but also psychologically. It's not that I was thinking, "Is this all there is?" I recognized my blessings. I love my children, and I was more than grateful for Paul and my boys. But still, I had so many things I wanted to do—I was worried that in some weird way, life was passing me by and, worse, would always pass me by.

That's how your mind can work when you fail to see the bigger picture. But the bigger picture was hard to find during those years when my idea of getting out of the house was strapping all the boys in their car seats, hitting a drive-through, and getting one extra-large Diet Coke all for me. The boys were so little that they didn't even know to ask for anything. Those were the days!

I'd get my drink, and we would drive into the country to look for horses and cows. And then we'd drive home and it would be nap time. I had one other regular outing—going to the park where I would meet friends for a playdate. After a while, however, I learned which parks we could handle and which ones offered too much open space and multiple escape routes for the Balducci boys. Eventually, even that was too much. I discovered that I was more than happy to meet friends at the fenced-in McDonald's play place (which was outside, so we did get fresh air). That was about it. Everything else was beyond me.

So that's where I was in life.

And then the boys started getting a little bigger and a little older. And before I knew it, I was down to just one boy at home with the three older brothers at school. Augie and I would hang out and go places, and a whole new world opened up for me. Of course, by then we were starting to have much more mobility than during those previous years, and I was feeling like a normal, contributing member of society once again.

Worries, averted. I was back!

Around that time, a dynamic priest was assigned to our parish. He needed help working on a Lenten reflection book, and I found myself very involved in helping build this book. I wanted to be part of this project because it was so much fun to be doing something outside the realm of chasing little boys. And I loved helping our parish. And this priest was so holy that I wanted to be a part of what he had going on.

It felt like a win-win all around. But in retrospect, I suspect that some of my worries and fear about missing out had crept back into my thinking. I had the opportunity to break out of my routine, and I seized it without too much thought. You can guess what happened. Little by little, that yes to the book led to another commitment, which led to something else. And before long I was in too deep, committed to projects for which I had no time or energy. Just like that, my yes went from a small, manageable commitment to opportunity overload.

That was my first taste of overcommitment. One pleasant side effect of all the small children was that they were a natural buffer against the temptation to do too much beyond staying alive and keeping them fed and clothed. But I was amazed at how quickly that changed just by starting to get involved.

We can't blame people for asking us to help. That's just a part of life. We can't manage overcommitment by waiting for fewer opportunities. Opportunities can be wonderful things, and life is filled with good things to do.

The key to a balanced life is developing the ability to recognize when worry and fear have become key factors in our decision-making process. For me, getting involved made me feel like I was a part of something. It's good to feel like you are a part of something—but not if you continue to say yes because you are afraid of being left out. Fear of missing out is a real problem for some people, and learning to identify it, especially in making decisions, will bring unending freedom and joy.

Learn to be honest about how you are handling your commitments. Sometimes you can say yes, and things are going well—and then, after some time, you realize you actually aren't managing things that well at all. This can sneak up on you and your best bet is to remedy the situation as soon as possible.

Fear Factor: Social Media

Making decisions out of fear, while it sounds terrible, is pretty understandable. It's exacerbated, though, by our constant exposure to people's lives on Facebook and Instagram. It can make us feel incredible pressure to keep up.

Social media gives us too deep a view into other people's yeses. We don't have any idea, usually, what they're saying no to, and it doesn't matter. When we see what they're doing, it's tempting to try to keep up. We want what they have— their travels, homes, volunteer activities, or stuff they do with their kids. We don't want to fall behind. If they can do that and have that, so can I! So *should* I.

Even before social media, though, this twisted type of motivation was a force. But social media has a way of putting all these feelings on steroids.

When our oldest son, Ethan, was four years old, I decided he needed to play soccer. After all, many of the people I followed on social media were putting their kids in organized sports at an even earlier age. Maybe I had already fallen behind! I was worried that if we didn't get him into sports at a young age, he wouldn't stand a chance when he got older. We signed him up for the Y soccer league so that he would have the advantages he needed when he got to middle school.

Never mind that at this time of my life, I was pregnant and also chasing a toddler. It was nuts. The whole scene. Every game involved a pack of tiny humans running up and down a field, possibly chasing after the ball, though I doubt any of them knew that. They knew all the other kids were running and so they had better keep up.

And me, my giant pregnant, exhausted self, was also running up and down the field. I was chasing after my toddler and pretty sure I saw less than 10 percent of what was going on in the game.

That soccer season felt like a bust. It was fun, on some level, but most of my thoughts revolved around the question, "What was the point of that?"

My husband takes a different approach to organized sports, having grown up in a time when children began to play sports when they turned nine or even later. He wasn't worried about Ethan at all. In fact, he tried to talk me out of putting Ethan into the league but was happy to coach when he saw that I was committed.

The result of that soccer season was that we didn't do organized sports for about five years after that. It wasn't worth it. Ethan and his brothers have all gone on to be wonderful athletes who have loved soccer and basketball but also many other activities as well, including music, scouting, and wood carving. They're well-rounded individuals.

This situation turned into an unforgettable lesson about anxiety-based decision making and also about trying to live up to other peoples' experiences. It became clear that hauling my kids to certain activities because I was worried about the future was not a great use of my time and energy.

On the other hand, if you love these activities, that's awesome. You should go for it! But if you find yourself exhausted and watching the clock tick down, it's okay to admit that this isn't working for you. Don't fear the future, and don't stretch yourself to burnout just because you are worried about your child not stacking up sometime down the road.

Fear of missing out is exhausting. Don't let it write your calendar.

A few years after the soccer exhaustion, we started to think about activities we might like to join. We had dinner with some friends—a couple who got married the same year as we did and were now a homeschooling family with eight children. My plan was to pick their brains to glean their wisdom. What perfect formula had they created to manage all the moving parts of their life?

It turns out that there wasn't a formula. This family knew they couldn't do everything and so they figured out exactly what they could do. They didn't have official equations such as one activity per child per season. Even more, I could see that they had no interest in measuring themselves against what other homeschooling families were doing. They were free, and their decision making reflected that.

That conversation inspired me and set for me a standard of doing what worked best for our family. It's a theme I've had to repeat to myself often, especially when I've been tempted to compare or be fearful.

Don't let a fear of missing out rule your life. As a child of God, you have freedom, so act with confidence. "For freedom Christ set us free" (Galatians 5:1). We are not slaves to fear or to worry or to pressure. God has a plan for you. Trust in him. Do what you love and what you can handle, but don't do anything simply because someone else is doing it and because you're afraid to be left behind.

THREE TIPS

1. Don't be afraid to let go of your plans as you open yourself to what God has in store for you.
2. When you pray for wisdom as you make decisions, consider if you are willing to say yes because you don't want to miss out. If that's the case, be willing to say no.
3. When trying to make decisions, don't compare yourself to those around you.

PERSONAL REFLECTION

1. When I make decisions, do I have the freedom to do what works best for me and for my family? Or am I committing to things only because it's what those around me are doing?
2. When I feel overloaded and burned out, does a fear of missing out contribute to that?

3. What steps can I take to avoid making decisions out of fear?

MOMENT OF GRACE

Prayer Tip

For many years, we tried, here and there, to say the Rosary as a family. It didn't work. I have friends who are able to pull this off, and even though it's a bit of a three-ring circus, they push through and just do it.

I never had the patience for wrestling too many monkeys while trying to pray. I found that just getting through our petitions and basic prayers was about all I could handle. And the fruit of that was really good.

And then some time went by, and the kids got a little older. We started trying the Rosary as a family prayer, and I have to say that the fruit was incredible. So I feel torn mentioning this because on the one hand, I don't think any of us should feel pressure or guilt about doing "the perfect" form of prayer. There is no perfect way. And if that's not where you are at, it could rob you of the very peace you are working to get. Don't try saying a family Rosary because you think you have to or that your family won't be holy if you don't.

But if you have the grace and peace to do it, go for it! Once we were able to say a Rosary without a meltdown (mine), it became a worthwhile endeavor.

The Rosary really is an incredible weapon and tool.

Prayer Starter

Litany of Humility

O Jesus, meek and humble of heart,
Hear me.
From the desire of being esteemed,
Deliver me, O Jesus.
From the desire of being loved,
Deliver me, O Jesus.
From the desire of being extolled,
Deliver me, O Jesus.
From the desire of being honored,
Deliver me, O Jesus.
From the desire of being praised,
Deliver me, O Jesus.
From the desire of being preferred to others,
Deliver me, O Jesus.
From the desire of being consulted,
Deliver me, O Jesus.
From the desire of being approved,
Deliver me, O Jesus.
From the fear of being humiliated,
Deliver me, O Jesus.
From the fear of being despised,
Deliver me, O Jesus.
From the fear of suffering rebukes,
Deliver me, O Jesus.
From the fear of being calumniated,
Deliver me, O Jesus.

From the fear of being forgotten,
Deliver me, O Jesus.
From the fear of being ridiculed,
Deliver me, O Jesus.
From the fear of being wronged,
Deliver me, O Jesus.
From the fear of being suspected,
Deliver me, O Jesus.

That others may be loved more than I,
Jesus, grant me the grace to desire it.
That others may be esteemed more than I,
Jesus, grant me the grace to desire it.
*That, in the opinion of the world, others may increase and
I may decrease,*
Jesus, grant me the grace to desire it.
That others may be chosen and I set aside,
Jesus, grant me the grace to desire it.
That others may be praised and I go unnoticed,
Jesus, grant me the grace to desire it.
That others may be preferred to me in everything,
Jesus, grant me the grace to desire it.
*That others may become holier than I, provided that I may
become as holy as I should,*
Jesus, grant me the grace to desire it.

—Cardinal Merry del Val[18]

CHAPTER SIX

The Value of Sabbath Rest and Why It's Often Overlooked

"He rested on the seventh day" (Genesis 2:2).

The idea of observing the Sabbath is based on the story of creation, found in the Book of Genesis. In it, we read that God created the world and its creatures in six days, and on the seventh day, he took a break. He rested. And so we have this notion that observing the Sabbath basically means that we have this one day—Sunday—when we don't work.

If we limit ourselves to that idea of the Sabbath, though, we rob ourselves of the true meaning of the day and of the reset that comes with taking a break. We need a rest, and not just from commuting to the office or from another day of labor. We do need a break physically, but we need one mentally and spiritually as well.

> Just as God "rested on the seventh day from all his work which he had done,"[19] human life has a rhythm of work and rest. The institution of the Lord's Day helps everyone enjoy adequate rest and leisure to cultivate their familial, cultural, social, and religious lives.[20] (*Catechism of the Catholic Church*, 2184)

Welcoming the Sabbath

I used to think that observing the Sabbath meant sitting around quietly reading books about saints. Or something like that. Anything else wasn't a true Sabbath.

But now I know that honoring the Sabbath means laying down our cares—making an effort to reset and catch our breath. It certainly means inviting God into the center of it as we rest from the work that wears us down. We put aside our cares and concerns and focus on goodness, peace, and joy—the gifts and life of God.

One way to get in a sabbath frame of mind is to welcome the Lord's Day with a little ceremony or time of prayer. It's a practical approach that marks the next twenty-four hours as a holy and relaxing time.

I grew up in a family that welcomed the Lord's Day on Saturday evening. At dinnertime, we gathered around the table, and my father distributed copies of a Lord's Day celebration that contained a set group of Scripture readings as well as prayers and responses that we prayed together. We made sure our relationships with other family members were in order. That meant that if I had done something unkind to a sibling, now was my opportunity to apologize. If I felt like something was not right between me and another family member, I could address it. It didn't happen often, but knowing there was this opportunity to set things straight was comforting. After that, we passed around a cup of wine (my favorite part), and we would each take a sip. We would have our turn to toast the Lord's goodness and, before taking our sip, say what we were thankful for.

After that, my mom lit a candle to signify Jesus as the light of the world, and my dad passed around a loaf of bread. We each tore off a small piece and, when everyone had their piece, held it up high and said, "To Jesus!" in unison.

And then we said the blessing and ate.

It was a simple but beautiful way to welcome the Sabbath, and it signaled to me, even as a child, the sacred nature of the day. Perhaps we wouldn't sit around all day Sunday (which sounds super boring to a child and super amazing to an adult), but even with this simple practice of "welcoming the Lord's day," I knew that this day was special.

When Paul and I got married and our kids were a little older, we decided to do our best to observe this same tradition. We have a nice meal on Saturday evening, and we start by lighting a candle, passing a cup of wine, sharing a loaf of bread, and toasting the Lord's goodness.

One week, only two of the children were at home, and I was heading out at dinnertime. We still stood in the kitchen, and I lit a candle. Then Paul poured a small cup of wine, we toasted the Lord, and we welcomed the Sabbath, and it was beautiful and good. Simple but profound.

Welcoming the Sabbath is a wonderful first step in honoring it. And then there is the actual day, the day of rest, whatever that means for each one of us.

Keeping the Sabbath

A few years ago, Paul decided to become a corporate sponsor of a local polo league. Every Sunday, we load up the family and head out on the thirty-minute drive to the polo fields. It has become an event that Paul and I love and treasure. Basically, it involves sitting for three hours and watching horses fly up and down a grass field. We eat good food and drink nice wine and chat with the people whose seats are next to ours. One of the couples that sit near us are Episcopalians, and when we all meet up at polo, they have just finished their church service and we've finished Mass. It's a beautiful way for us to enjoy ecumenical friendship.

Paul said it best when he described this outing as the perfect way to "sabbath."

It's been a blessing, and we come home renewed and ready for a new week. We haven't spent the day running errands or working around the house. We have rested.

Now, here's a beautiful thing about the Sabbath: you can decide what is relaxing for you. The key is to make sure you are inviting God into your day and laying down whatever burdens you can.

Another important aspect of the Sabbath, according to the *Catechism*, is the call to avoid burdening those who must work due to poverty or other life circumstances.

Those Christians who have leisure should be mindful of their brethren who have the same needs and the same rights, yet cannot rest from work because of poverty and misery. Sunday is traditionally consecrated by Christian piety to good works and humble service of the sick, the infirm, and the elderly. Christians will also sanctify Sunday by devoting time and care to their families and relatives, often difficult to do on other days of the week. (2186)

Family time on the Sabbath is especially important because the rest of the week can be so hectic. We set aside time to be together as a family because it is often difficult to do on other days of the week.

One other way to welcome Sunday as a day of rest is to have a "protected time" during each day of the week. When I was growing up, my parents didn't answer the phone or let us come and go during the dinner hour. This was our time—just an hour or two—where we were striving for uninterrupted time together. Consider turning off phones and avoiding all internet activity for at least a few hours on the Lord's Day.

It's so tricky to live like this if you are out of the habit. These days, we feel compelled to check our phones constantly and be available 24/7, but it doesn't need to be this way—at least not on the Sabbath. If you can get in the habit of setting boundaries with the internet, with your phone, and with people coming and going so that you can focus on the task at hand—eating a meal in peace, for example—that can relieve some of the stress during the rest of the week when you feel pulled in too many directions with no end in sight. Protected time creates boundaries that will go a long way toward helping you live the abundant life.

Setting limits like these or having hard stops in the day reminds me of the Liturgy of the Hours, those prayers said by monks and religious and some laypeople too at different times of the day. The Liturgy of the Hours makes the day revolve around prayer—you might want to choose a couple of those prayer times on Sundays to help you keep your focus on the Lord. There are many books and websites that

But we can see prayer as the *heart of our day* and not something we squeeze in to relieve our guilt.

keep track of the hours and days, making it easy to dip into this ancient prayer practice.

I returned to volunteering with the Missionaries of Charity when our youngest, Isabel, was old enough to come along. What I noticed, returning all those years later, was that prayer is the central focus of the sisters' days. They don't fit prayer into their schedule. They fit their schedule into prayer. That's how they are able to do everything they do with such peace and joy. They see the actions of their day as an extension of their relationship with Jesus. The time they spend at his feet is the fuel that fires their activity.

These stops in the day—bringing the focus back to God and his love for us and his plans for each one of us—this confirms the notion of the Sabbath. It's taking a break and stepping back to regroup.

We have that same access to the Lord and to his goodness. We might not be able to pray seven times a day, but we can see prayer as the heart of our day and not something we squeeze in to relieve our guilt. Observing the Sabbath, that reset and time of prayer, can remind us that everything we do is done for the Lord and in his power. We can face down the week knowing that we are in the center of God's will.

If I start my week giving everything to God and then spend each day giving it to him again, I can't go wrong. I take a step back when I feel tired and overwhelmed, and I try to lay my burden down. And I remember that even if I feel tired and overwhelmed, this too shall pass. I can push myself hard today and maybe for the next few days, because I know a rest is coming.

And then when that rest arrives, when the Sabbath gets here, I must take advantage of it. I have to choose to embrace that day and let God give me the rest I need. That's how we keep going and manage all we have going on.

The Sabbath is God's way of reminding us that he is with us and for us, and with him we are managing just fine. Even when the days feel a little crazy, he offers us this reset so that we can rest in him and find peace and confidence and learn to trust in him.

A "Sabbath" Approach to Decision Making

The concept of sabbath rest applies not only to our weekly schedule, but also to our attitude as we consider our commitments. In other words, we are in tune with the Holy Spirit because we are spending time in prayer and putting our plans, desires, and dreams into God's hands.

But what about those times when we do pray but don't find peace? When we can't get a handle on what we're supposed to do?

This is a perfect time to apply a "sabbath" attitude within a unique situation. It's a time to adapt the notion of sabbath rest in order to approach decision making in peace. On the Sabbath, we step away from our burdens. In "sabbath" decision making, we step away from the decision making and think about something else.

Trying to make a decision can feel like carrying around a bag of bricks. It's so heavy a load that it's all we can think about. When I start to feel this way, I know it's time for me to shelve the decision for a time in order to take a break.

That can be easier said than done. I find the process pretty scary, to be honest. Generally, if I'm giving something this much thought, it means I need to come up with a plan. And usually, if the decision is demanding so much of my attention, I need to formulate that plan pretty quickly.

Recently, I concluded that I needed to take my own advice and take a sabbath approach to decision making. It took me a while, though, to come to that conclusion. My husband and I were trying to help our high school senior decide his plans for the next year. College? Gap year? Working full-time? Doing volunteer work? We floated all of those ideas around one morning on our four-minute ride to school. We said our quick prayers—petitions, one Hail Mary, and one St. Michael the Archangel—and then the discussion began.

And just like that, I realized that we had some big decisions to make. And we were a little behind. Lots of other high school seniors were about to find out exactly what they would be doing next year (because we were a few weeks away from early acceptance letters), but I wasn't going to let that get me down. All I could do was focus on supporting my son, the only high school senior out there that I was in charge of. I didn't want to compare or fret or worry about how this had to come together in some magical way.

To top it off, I was also working on a few career decisions of my own, trying to decide if I should go back to school as part of my new (and much-loved) job as a journalism professor at the local university. If I did that, it meant taking an entrance exam while also writing a book. It meant studying for the math (gulp) portion of the exam too. I had a lot to think about.

So on this particular afternoon of this particular day, I decided that I needed a Sabbath. I had to shelve the thoughts because they were quickly turning into frets. Fretting gets us nowhere, but it can tempt us. When faced with a big decision (or decisions), I tend to think constantly about all the details. I'm inclined to go over and over the options and what-ifs and how-tos. But the way of trust and love is best experienced by giving these variables to God.

"God," I said when I stopped by the small chapel near campus, "I'm overwhelmed. And I'm feeling sad, for some weird reason, which is usually an indication that my brain is tired. Can you please take this for me?"

And then, in those five minutes while I knelt in that small chapel, I mentally presented my package of worries and cares to the Lord. I set it before him and asked him to take it over for me. And then I asked if he would help me trust him in all of these decisions.

"Lord," I continued, "you are the Lord of my future plans and my kids' future plans too. Please guide us in all of this. Help me to rely on you, and please keep me from all fear and anxiety."

And then I walked out of the chapel and headed back to my office, free as a bird.

Kinda.

In reality, I first ran in to visit my colleague, whose office door was open. He asked how my day was going, and I unloaded all of these things that were on my mind—which proved to me that I hadn't really left them in that imaginary box at the feet of Jesus. I was embarrassed about being so honest and I apologized, and my colleague was really nice about it.

And then I realized that I needed to take a break from the decision. For real this time.

I tried a quick trip to the chapel, and I tried talking it through with a coworker. And when neither of those approaches fixed my worry, I knew I really needed to lay it down.

So every time the issue came into my head, I made a decision not to think about it. I asked the Lord to take the issue and hold on to it for me until it was the right time. Sometimes, I've found, you have to use this approach on repeat, until your brain decides to really let it go. We have the choice of what we allow to go through our minds, and I had to choose not to obsess.

"Lord please carry this for me until you can show us a plan," I said. "Until you give Paul and me the tools to help our son find the solution."

Just because you want to keep thinking about something doesn't mean you have to. Did you know that? It took me a while in life to figure it out, and this truth has brought me great joy and freedom. It applies to negative thinking and destructive thoughts, but it can also be used in times when you just don't have the right answer and when going over the details isn't propelling the situation.

So you step back and take a break. A sabbath break, if you will.

This doesn't mean we walk away from life or our problems. And that's what is so good about a Sabbath. In it, we find rest, knowing we will get back to our reality once the Sabbath is over.

And so it is with our decision making. We don't ignore it. We just put it aside for a time. It's a way of setting down the bag of bricks. We don't have to carry them with us everywhere we go. We set them down until we can manage the issue in a way that helps us move forward in peace.

THREE TIPS

1. Honor the Sabbath, and keep it a delight. Make sure to find time to rest.
2. If you have decisions to make and can't find peace, give them a small rest. Ask God to carry this load until it is time for you to manage it.
3. Find something you enjoy that brings you peace and joy, something fun and restorative. Find time on the Sabbath for this activity, maybe a family hike or a special meal together.

PERSONAL REFLECTION

1. Do I take time to honor the Lord's Day? Do I have a time of rest and relaxation built into my week?
2. What activities or cares keep me from finding time to take a break from the duties of the week?

MOMENT OF GRACE

Prayer Tip

One simple way to welcome the Lord's Day is to take a few minutes to toast the Lord for his goodness. Even if you don't have bread and wine to pass around, stop what you are doing and welcome the Sabbath.

Prayer Starter

Welcoming the Lord's Day

The woman lights a candle and says,
Blessed art thou, O Lord our God, King of the Universe, who has sanctified us and has commanded us to kindle the sabbath light.
Blessed art thou, O Lord our God, King of the Universe, who has given us thy only begotten Son, the light of the world.

The man lifts up a cup of wine and says,
Blessed art thou, O Lord our God, King of the Universe, who has created the fruit of the vine.

He then shares something he is thankful for and takes a sip of wine. The cup is passed around the table for others to do the same. The man holds up the loaf of bread and says,
Blessed art thou, O Lord our God, King of the Universe, who gives us the bread of the earth.

He takes a small piece from the loaf and passes the loaf around the table for others to do the same. Everyone holds the bread up and together says,
Blessed art Thou, O Lord our God, King of the Universe, who has given us this Sabbath.

CHAPTER SEVEN

What to Do When Asked to Serve

Have you ever noticed that certain activities energize you? Maybe it's even an activity that other people find totally stressful, like cooking for others or going for a big grocery trip. Or is that just me? Certain activities that seem pretty straightforward and basic for some people are downright stressful for others. And vice versa.

An opportunity that energizes and excites you instead of wearing you out might be something like singing in a choir or giving a talk or even volunteering for a charity. It takes time from your busy schedule, but it doesn't feel as if you are giving too much. In fact, you find that you actually get more than you give.

When you feel this way about certain activities, you are most likely expressing your charisms—those special gifts and abilities that God has given you to draw you and those you serve closer to him. The *Catechism* tells us that these gifts "are intended for the common good of the Church. They are at the service of charity which builds up the Church" (2003, cf. 1 Corinthians 12).

Every one of us has a charism or combination of charisms— no one is excluded. Your charisms could include mercy or wisdom or diplomacy or craftsmanship or any of the many gifts given by the Holy Spirit. You probably have some sense of your gifts—maybe you know you're good at administration or hospitality or leadership or intercessory prayer. Knowing what your charisms are can help you understand which tasks are more suited to your abilities and a more natural fit when you're trying to figure out what opportunities will work for you. Within your charisms, you will have a little more wiggle room for saying yes.

Some of that is a matter of learning as you go. Over time you might discover that what initially appears to be an epic request—a burden to you and your schedule—is actually pretty life-giving. You don't know until you try. Sometimes that's the only way to discover if it's an activity that totally depletes you or one that gives you life.

A few years ago, my friend Susie, who is a skilled nurse practitioner, mother of six, and downright super generous person, was asked to write an article for our community newsletter. She was stressed. As we talked, I couldn't figure out what the big deal was. "That should take you, like, twenty minutes," I said in an effort to encourage her.

Instead of feeling encouraged, she asked if I would write it for her. She offered to cook dinner for my family in exchange, and because cooking is low on my list of favorite activities (and writing is very high), she had a deal.

That's a funny example of putting our charisms at one another's service! We knew our gifts, and that helped to take the pressure off the situation. Understanding what we find tough to do versus what we find easy to do reminds us what we personally are equipped to do. We make our choices based on our gifts and our limits.

Sometimes, however, we know that saying yes is going to cost us something, but we still go for it. This is how I feel when I cook for people in need. Cooking stresses me out, mostly because I'm not the world's greatest cook, and I worry that that my food doesn't taste particularly good. But I don't say no. I don't let my insecurities rule me. I push through and say yes because there is a need.

Now, even with this kind of request, it's still important to have boundaries. I might not take on every single cooking request, but I have certain groups of people I will always say yes to, and I push through my feelings of inadequacy. Even if it's a bit of a pinch, for example, I am committed to making meals for anyone in our small prayer group, but not necessarily for someone at a neighboring parish.

I don't want to sound cruel or harsh—I just want to offer an example regarding how to make decisions about saying yes. Knowing your charisms—your gifts, your limits—helps fight the compulsion to want to do it all.

Where we get bogged down is when we start to say yes to every request for our time and resources. Still, it can be difficult to know how to proceed because the requests we receive often reflect a deep need. If there is a real need and you are certain there is no one else to stand in the gap, it's worth the effort to sign on, even if it pushes you outside of your comfort zone. But if you are in the habit of saying yes to everything, and there are lots of others also willing to help, it's okay to step back and let someone else do it.

A few years ago, I was asked to make a meal for a mother on a citywide sports team, a team with hundreds of kids. At the same time, there was a need for meals for a family in our neighborhood. I couldn't do both, so I opted to cook for the family nearby. I knew this request was going out to a smaller pool and that fewer people would be asked to help. It was more important to say yes to that neighborhood situation than to jump in at the citywide level.

Remember: it's okay to step back and consider the situation. We have to examine where we are in life and our own circumstances when we are in the midst of responding to others' needs. We consider what else we have going on before we decide exactly where and how to commit.

The Inconvenience of Sacrifice

This is where the conversation can start to feel tricky, and perhaps even selfish. People have needs and we have abilities, and the two should meet!

Let's go back to the basics: God has given each of us specific gifts, he has a plan, and we are learning to be in tune with what he wants us to do. We can be at peace in the midst of that. But being open and willing to serve is not only key, it's also an important element of basic Christian living. A willingness to serve keeps our problems in perspective. It takes our minds off ourselves and all we have going on, and reminds us to focus on those around us.

God makes it clear in Scripture that using our particular gifts and serving others is a necessary component of our Christian life.

> Since we have gifts that differ according to the grace given
> to us, let us exercise them: if prophecy, in proportion to the

faith; if ministry, in ministering; if one is a teacher, in teaching; if one exhorts, in exhortation; if one contributes, in generosity; if one is over others, with diligence; if one does acts of mercy, with cheerfulness. (Romans 12:6-8)

I once heard a talk in which the speaker described service as a two-way street: "We meet a need and we grow out of our own self-interest. It creates a heart to give." We have to be willing to serve, the speaker added, and we must "give ourselves permission to be inconvenienced."

I love this concept—the willingness to be inconvenienced. We can all agree that it's easy to have a calendar and to-do list that's so jam-packed that there's no wiggle room for anything extra. But we need to allow ourselves the time to serve others. We can do so—we can give ourselves permission to be inconvenienced—when we have an ordered day. When we are in tune with the promptings of the Holy Spirit, we are open to being guided where he needs us to go.

Practically speaking, of course, we need to find that balance. Some of us might struggle with being too quick to say yes to a request for service, but some of us might be too quick to say no. Personally, I've learned that if the request is something bigger than helping run a carpool or cook a meal for someone, I talk to Paul before I commit. This buys me time and allows me to say either yes or no out of freedom and not out of a misguided attempt to make people happy.

In the past, I've committed to what sounded like a small act of service only to discover it was way more than I anticipated. Conversely, there are times when something sounds really overwhelming and epic, and it turns out to be not a big deal at all and might even be a blessing.

When Isabel was a toddler (which meant Henry was in kindergarten and I had four boys in middle and high school), I got a call from an elderly woman at our parish. Mrs. Lewis was the secretary of her garden club, and because I wrote a column for our diocesan paper, she was wondering if I might be able to help her make a flier for their upcoming luncheon.

Of course, I would not. That was my immediate response.

I didn't tell Mrs. Lewis this, not yet. I decided to tell Paul about it so that I could be affirmed in my obvious decision to tell her that no way do I have time for this. I fully expected Paul to tell me not to even think twice about saying yes. And instead, he said, "Maybe you should see what she needs."

I realized that in my automatic negative response, I hadn't stopped to consider that it might be something I could handle. At the very least, it was worth hearing what she was looking for.

It was all very old school, this situation. We spoke on the phone (instead of texting), and I drove to her house (instead of emailing), and she showed me the printed photos (instead of digital) that she wanted included in her program. Someone with basic computer skills could have handled what she was looking for. It was a simple request—type up names and information, and get a few dozen programs printed.

My thoughts were twofold. On one hand, I am way over-qualified for this task. On the other, this is way above my skill set. I'm a writer, not a graphic artist. I stink at this sort of thing!

But Mrs. Lewis was so sweet. And I thought about the fact that I didn't know very many people from the early Sunday

Mass we both went to. At that point, I only knew other families with kids, young parents who also bided their time in the cry room with sniveling babies.

So I told Mrs. Lewis I would be happy to help, but I also let her know there were people out there who could make this program look way better than I could. I didn't have a graphic design degree, but I had enough basic skills to get the job done.

Because the boys were all in school, the project involved Isabel and me making several trips to see Mrs. Lewis to pick up the pictures and information, to bring her the rough draft, and to finally get the finished product from the print shop and over to her.

In the midst of our visits, I learned that Mrs. Lewis, who always attended Mass with her grown daughter, had raised eight very successful children. She was widowed at a young age and the year before that had lost a daughter who was still a little girl. Suddenly, this little old lady I would see in the pew each week became a real, live person with a rich history. Mrs. Lewis was a total queen.

Mrs. Lewis is still very special to me and Isabel. Each week at the end of Mass, we walk over to her and give her a hug. Mrs. Lewis and her daughter came to Isabel's First Communion, and I have the loveliest picture of the two of them— Isa in her flowing dress and Mrs. Lewis in her best Sunday hat. Isa is devoted to Mrs. Lewis and still has the little stuffed animal that she gave her.

All of this because I listened to Paul and decided to just see what Mrs. Lewis needed, and then took a hard look at whether or not I could help.

So yes, sometimes we say yes to things that on paper don't make sense. And this is where being open to the Holy Spirit and the voice of wise people in your life comes in handy. It didn't hurt for me to see what Mrs. Lewis needed, and while it was a very slight inconvenience, the fruit of that yes yielded a warm friendship that also made me feel more connected by my parish.

The Joy of Saying Yes

The first summer I was able to return to the Missionaries of Charity as a mom with children, I found volunteering to be a stretch.

I brought my three youngest children with me—they were eight, eleven, and sixteen at the time. We stayed at the home of a couple who were benefactors of the sisters. The home was about five miles from the convent but about a twenty-minute drive in traffic.

Every morning we left at 6:30 for Mass. Then we stayed and had breakfast before heading out with the sisters to the apartment complex where they ran their summer camp for children.

My older son helped as a counselor, while my youngest two joined their age group as campers.

They loved it.

They made friends with children whose life circumstances were totally different from theirs, and they learned that happiness and joy are universal emotions. Bringing your children to serve the "less fortunate" is not at all about making your kids grateful for the stuff they have. It's about learning that life is so much bigger than stuff and things, and that in order to be fully human we need to love those around us.

As for me, sometimes I was tempted to focus on what a pain it was to drive in big-city traffic or how staying in someone's basement was way less fun than being at home. I was tempted to focus on being away from Paul for a week and on giving up a week of my time to play games and sing songs and make beaded necklaces. Being home and doing my thing is definitely more convenient! But that's the beauty of service—it's not about what's convenient; it's about being the hands and feet of Jesus.

And honestly, those thoughts were fleeting because the minute I jumped into real, wholehearted generosity, it was pretty contagious. Spending a week volunteering with my children drew us all out of our own wants and desires and schedules (which can become like little gods) and into giving.

One of the highlights of that time was seeing how God used our yeses to him in such unexpected ways. A few days before we left for the week, I found out that two women from a Catholic college would be staying at the house with us. They were flying up from Florida and would tag along with me and my children in our van. By the end of that week, we were smitten with those young ladies. They were a beautiful part of our experience with the sisters, and they said the same about us.

A few weeks after we got home, I got a wonderful letter from them: "We wanted to thank you for taking such good care of us all week—we wouldn't have been able to do the camp without you, so THANK YOU. Thanks for everything—for McDonald's runs, the park and market, laughs,

Generosity to those around us is *transformative*. It changes us in the midst of changing those we serve.

understanding, and every joy-filled moment in between. With love . . . "—signed, the girls.

My yes to working at the camp helped them with their yeses. Practically, they needed rides, and we were able to help. Isn't it humbling when we get to see what our yes means to someone else, how it really can bless those around us?

Generosity to those around us is transformative. It changes us in the midst of changing those we serve. For all our discussion on boundaries and burnout and overcommitment, let's remember this: we can't outgive God.

THREE TIPS

1. Being willing to serve is essential.
2. Let God use you as his hands and feet. You never know when you might be the answer to someone else's prayer.
3. Prayerfully consider requests to serve. Be open to saying yes, but have a plan for making the right decision.

PERSONAL REFLECTION

1. Am I generous with my time when asked to serve?
2. What obstacles prevent me from feeling free to say yes when asked to help others?
3. Do I have a way of making sure that I am free to say yes without guilt, but that I am not too quick to say no?

MOMENT OF GRACE

Prayer Tip

Praying for others is an important way we build the body of Christ. How do we follow through when we tell others we are "praying for them"? Get in the habit some time during the day to offer up the sufferings and petitions of others. Make a list you keep on the refrigerator or somewhere handy. I know several families who keep Christmas cards in a place where they regularly pull the cards out to pray for those families. Praying for others is an important way of keeping our minds off ourselves, and that is a freeing way to live.

Prayer Starter

Radiating Christ

Dear Jesus, help me to spread Your fragrance wherever I go.

Flood my soul with Your spirit and life. Penetrate and possess my whole being so utterly,
That my life may only be a radiance of Yours.

Shine through me, and be so in me that every soul I come in contact with may feel Your presence in my soul. Let them look up and see no longer me, but only Jesus! Stay with me, and then I shall begin to shine as You shine, so as to be a light to others.

The light, O Jesus, will be all from You; none of it will be mine. It will be you, shining on others through me. Let me thus praise You the way You love best, by shining on those around me.

Let me preach You without preaching, not by words but by my example, by the catching force of the sympathetic influence of what I do, the evident fullness of the love my heart bears to You. Amen.

—St. John Henry Newman[21]

CHAPTER EIGHT

Considering Long-Term Commitments

I'm going to start this chapter by telling you a story. But I warn you, it's a sad story, and it might make you dislike me or like me a little less than before. I want to tell you this story because it's proof that sometimes, when we know we are overcommitted and in over our heads, we have to do difficult things for our own sanity. I had to make a choice—an extremely difficult choice—about a really cute puppy who turned into a dog who could not behave. The story involves that dog, my kids, and me—a very tired and overwhelmed version of me—and a ton of tears.

You see, in this particular season of life, I decided that what our family really needed was a dog. I don't know where the feeling came from, but I can tell you now it was not the Holy Spirit. I was motivated, I think, by wanting to give my children something—warm childhood memories, maybe, centered on having a family pet. I thought about the joy a dog would bring and the sense of responsibility the children would develop as they helped take care of it.

Mostly, I envisioned my beautiful children running around with a dog, the dog's tongue hanging wildly to one side, everyone smiling and laughing. I saw us all sitting on the floor in the front room, one of the boys snuggled up with the dog and us living our best, front-room family life.

And then one day a magazine came in the mail and on the cover was the most gorgeous litter of hunting dogs. I knew I had to have one. *We* had to have one.

You might wonder how I could possibly make such a permanent and huge decision because of a cute picture of some really cute dogs on a magazine cover. I don't quite know, but that's basically what happened.

One afternoon a few weeks before Christmas, I loaded our six children into the van, and we drove out into the country, about an hour from our home. I had heard of a woman who sold the exact kind of dog I had seen on the magazine cover. She lived in a trailer in the woods and had multiple litters of tiny cute puppies roaming around her home, under a sofa, under a chair, and into the kitchen. It was pretty crazy.

Looking back, I realize it might not have been the best idea to buy a puppy from someone who had been breeding these dogs for years from the same stock—inbreeding them, essentially: doggie aunts and uncles and moms and dads all living in this trailer together. I'm only mentioning that because fast-forward almost two years, and we had made it through the difficult part of having a puppy. Now we had a fully grown dog (just about) who still had no idea how to behave. I started to wonder if the dog was simply not capable of being trained.

Beyond that, I realized that I had made a terrible mistake. I bought a dog out of emotion and without consulting my husband (which generally is a bad way to do business in my home), and two years in, the children ate breakfast sitting on the kitchen countertops because the dog wouldn't quit stealing their food. I knew I had to do something because the stress was overwhelming. At that point, our daughter was almost two and our five sons ranged in age from five to fourteen. It was all too much.

The story ends in a wonderful way because our neighbors across the street were happy to take our dog for us. We were able to visit him regularly, and he was happy. The neighbors were happy, and I was really, really happy. But it was also one of the hardest decisions I had ever had to make at that point in my parenting career. If that sounds like an exaggeration, believe me when I say it was not. I had taken this precious puppy, brought him into our home and into our world, and had made him part of our pack. And then, when I was finally able to admit that it was a bad idea, I had to break the news to our children. It was gut-wrenching.

I'm not asking you to make a call on my decision. I did what I needed to do, but when I wrote about it on my blog, as it all went down, I got a lot of hate mail. It was tough.

Nevertheless, I want to tell you this story because part of living a life of true freedom and peace is being allowed to say, "I made a mistake. This is more than I can handle." We can't do that with everything, of course, but we can do it with plenty.

It's important to have wisdom going into big (and small) decisions, but when we miss the boat, sometimes we have to have the courage to admit it. There will be times when what you signed up for is more than you realized it would be or it has gone on longer than you anticipated, and you no longer have the grace for it. When that happens, you must have the

It's important to have *wisdom* going into big (and small) decisions, but when we miss the boat, sometimes we have to have the *courage* to admit it.

freedom to admit it and the wisdom to walk away. And you will learn from the experience so that you don't keep finding yourself in situations that drag you down.

So how do you avoid making these mistakes? That's an important question because even though you might be able to pull the plug, you don't want to get into the habit of making big commitments that consistently backfire.

So what do you do?

- Make sure you are saying yes out of freedom.
- If you are married, make sure you talk through your considerations with your spouse.
- If it's a really big deal, ask a good friend or a spiritual advisor for further feedback.
- Think of the nonnegotiables in your life—your family and your sanity—and be sure that they can withstand this new endeavor and long-term commitment if you decide to go for it.

In essence, you should proceed with caution, but you should also keep in mind the frequent advice of Pope St. John Paul II: "Do not be afraid."[22] Because it's important to be open to something beyond what you consider the realm of the possible. It might be something that actually works out.

Crossroads and Commitment

When Paul and I had been married for only a year, I had this really wild idea: I'd study for my master's degree at the university a few hours away. It wasn't a long-term commitment, really, but it felt like it was in the context of life as a newly-wed. It would involve one year of coursework on campus, and then I could conduct research and write my thesis from home. While it was short-term in the grand scheme, it was a big commitment at the time.

It felt like an insane idea, so I proceeded cautiously, one small step at a time.

First, I discussed it with Paul. He loved the idea.

Next, I studied for the entrance exam and took that. And I passed!

A few days later, I applied to the program. And I got in!

Then, we drove up to the university and started looking at housing for me. We had no money and Paul was just starting his own law practice. We decided that he would stay in Augusta in the fixer-upper we had just bought and would continue to build his practice. I would live in the college town and come home on weekends when I was able.

I applied for housing but wound up on a waiting list for the graduate dorms, which is what we could afford. In the meantime, I could live in the giant undergrad high-rise dorms if I wanted, which I didn't want at all. At that point, I was a twenty-three-year-old married woman who figured that living with a crop of recent high school graduates wouldn't be a great fit. I went to visit the dorm and it only confirmed my suspicions.

I found a room to rent, but after a few days of trying to commute to campus on a bike—our only car was back home with Paul—I knew that wasn't going to work. One afternoon, after I narrowly escaped a bus on a bike ride to campus, I went back to student housing to see if, by chance, a room had opened up at the graduate dorm. The person at the desk was hanging up the phone as I walked in. Someone had just canceled her slot in the very dorm where I hoped to stay.

"Let me guess," the man said. "You want a room in the graduate dorm." And he gave me that spot.

And just like that, I knew God had ever so gently opened every single door I needed opened in that season. Something that seemed a little out there—moving away right after my first anniversary—came together with ease and peace. First and foremost, my husband was on board, and from there the details all came together.

That's when we know we are moving in the right direction. Sometimes we try to make things work, and it feels as if we're fighting an uphill battle. That's usually a sign to me that this isn't what I'm supposed to be doing, especially when it involves a long-term commitment. That's not to say we give up at the first sign of tension, but that we are willing to let it go when there is no grace or peace and when we feel all stirred up inside.

Sometimes too we add to the confusion by creating questions that aren't quite related to the matter at hand. We overcomplicate matters. We think the options are A or B, for example, when it's possible that those options are not mutually exclusive.

Maybe you can do both A and B, but not exactly at the same time.

A few years ago, I was at a crossroads. I had a new book coming out, and the publisher's marketing plan was excellent and well-executed. I knew I could come up with a series of talks and presentations that would help promote the book on a large scale. I started gathering contact information for interviews and endorsements, and I updated my website.

In the meantime, out of the blue, a woman contacted me and asked me to speak at a retreat she was organizing. The topic for my talk was the very topic for one of the talks I had mentally created for my marketing plan, but I hadn't written it yet and had told no one about it. I felt that this was a sign that I was on the right track. Around that same time, a part-time job opportunity arose. And therein started the handwringing.

One door had opened: presenting a talk that I had hoped to do everywhere! But another door had opened as well: teaching adjunct at the local university! I loved both options.

And instead of just saying yes to both, I started to over-think it. A lot. Like all the time. "So what will I do?" I ruminated constantly. "Will I pursue a full-time speaking career? Or a full-time teaching career? How will I choose? What will that look like?"

I won't lie. I obsessed about the choice I was sure I had to make. Except, there really wasn't a choice. I had one speaking offer and one adjunct offer to teach two classes, and that was it. But I was acting as if I was being asked to speak all the time at a national level or commit to a long-term, full-time university career.

I was talking about this with my dad one day—which door I should go through, and how would I know and, most important, why was this causing me so much stress?—and he hit the nail on the head. "I think you're trying to choose a door, to go through a door, that isn't even there."

And that was the truth. I was fretting about a decision I didn't have to make. I was trying to think about things so far down the road that I couldn't get traction. I couldn't make a decision because there wasn't one to make. So I said yes to that one-day retreat and also to the adjunct faculty opportunity. And it was all very manageable.

When I quit trying to figure everything out, I knew exactly what I needed to do.

Don't overthink it.

That might sound counter to pretty much every other thing I've said in this book. We have to be open and prayerful and ask God to direct us. We have to consider all the things we have going on in life and think about it all. And we have to be willing to serve and to be inconvenienced. But mostly, we have to take it all in stride.

The minute any of this feels like a burden, set it aside. If you are working so hard to find peace that you are robbing yourself of peace, give yourself some room. Or find a trusted friend or spiritual director or, even better, your dad, who listens to you and tells you it's going to work out—and also, that you might need to calm your bad self down.

THREE TIPS

1. Think through long-term commitments.
2. Don't overthink them.
3. Try to find a balance between tip one and tip two, for therein lies your sanity.

PERSONAL REFLECTION

1. When it comes to making big decisions, do I have a channel for seeking wisdom and talking through options to help me arrive at a decision?
2. When I seek counsel before making decisions, am I willing to listen?
3. Am I peaceful with waiting before trying to decide about something that needs more time to develop?

MOMENT OF GRACE

Prayer Tip

I've mentioned that going to the Adoration chapel has been instrumental in my personal spiritual journey. A few thoughts on this: one, you really can take children to the Adoration chapel, and some children will last a little longer than others. Even stopping by while you are out doing some other errand is an excellent habit to get into. And personally, once I'm in the habit of stopping in even for five minutes, it quickly becomes something that stays on my radar.

Don't let perfection be the enemy of really excellent. Not everyone can do a Holy Hour weekly, but spending a few minutes of that quiet regularly is life changing. You can pray in quiet contemplation at home, too, of course, but when we are able to get before the Eucharist, incredible graces flow.

Prayer Starter

Prayer to the Holy Spirit

Come Holy Spirit, fill the hearts of your faithful.
And kindle in them the fire of your love.
Send forth your Spirit and they shall be created.
And You shall renew the face of the earth.

Lord, by the light of the Holy Spirit
You have taught the hearts of your faithful.
In the same Spirit
Help us to relish what is right
And always rejoice in your consolation.
We ask this through Christ Our Lord.
Amen.[23]

CHAPTER NINE

No Regrets—Moving Forward in Freedom

We can learn from our mistakes, and God can use all things to his glory. But one of the ways we can be overcommitted is by being too committed to our own plans. By now we can see that it's not going to work to map out what we think should happen, sign up to do something, get burned out, and then repeat the process over and over (and over!) again.

If I'm finding myself on a burnout shuffle—same old worn-out me, just a new venue—it's time to consider all the ways I'm doing it wrong. We don't want life to be about committing until we reach a breaking point and then having to start over again.

We can, however, let our past mistakes guide us, helping us acquire the insight we need to make the right decisions going forward.

Here's a little story along those lines. It involves my hair, which is maybe not what you were expecting, but there you go.

Years ago, after our initial baby-centric years, we didn't have a baby—we had a toddler and three older boys. I found myself, for the first time in quite some time, having time to think.

And what did I think about? Did I consider some grand new venture, or try to figure out a way to plug in more intentionally to the world around me? Nope. I settled on something way less lofty.

"

We can, however, let our past mistakes *guide us*, helping us acquire the insight we need to make the right decisions going forward.

I thought about how getting a pixie haircut would be the solution to all my problems.

I somehow settled on the image of a lovely young French actress who had recently received a lot of attention for shearing her locks and, as a result, bringing her gorgeous face into better focus.

I didn't get any input from others as I contemplated this move —I went blindly forward. I was sure, looking at that picture, that if I got the same haircut, it would transform me.

And transform me it did.

I won't save this part for the end of the story; I'm going to put it right up top. One out-of-town family member, seeing me for the first time with my new short hairdo, went back home to his wife and described me to her: "She looks like MacGyver."

Do you remember him? The star of the 1980s TV drama featuring that dude who could solve every problem with a paper clip and a ball of twine? Don't focus on his awesomeness—focus on his hairdo. That's what I looked like, according to our relative. His comment wasn't particularly soul crushing because by the time I got this feedback, I knew it was true.

This haircut looked terrible on me. It was awkward and embarrassing, and suddenly everything about my life "BC" (before the cut) seemed blissful and perfect. I literally don't know what I was thinking or what I ever had to worry about. That was before, and this was now. Everything had changed and the kind of attention you get for having a haircut like this—I don't recommend it.

I went to see a friend who has, for years now, rocked the most perfect pixie you ever saw. She told me what I already suspected: one, my hair had not been cut short enough for a proper pixie, and two, my hair really didn't want to be in a pixie. It had way too much going on in the thickness and cowlick departments.

"Please don't let me die with this haircut," I told Paul through tears when he first saw me.

By now I knew that I was, in fact, not a good candidate for a pixie. So while there was no turning back, I also wasn't going to go back. There was no need to return to my hairdresser and have more taken off because this cut was never going to work for me. This would be Day One of Growing Out Hair, a season that ended up taking just shy of two years to complete.

It was a painful time.

So what did I learn from all that, and what does it have to do with being overcommitted?

Well, one, I know that I will never ever (ever!) come close to trying that hairdo again. No matter what existential crisis I'm experiencing, that haircut will not solve my problems. So I learned one of those valuable, painful lessons that you can only learn by walking through it.

Two, and more important, I will get multiple opinions before I make a sudden move. I will ask people what they think, and I will be open to hearing what they have to say.

A few months ago, I was getting a similar crazy idea—maybe cutting a few inches off my hair would make life easier. I texted my sister and I mentioned it to my hairdresser (a new hairdresser by now) and both answered with a resounding "NO!" Yes, I'm free to do what I please, but the pain of that pixie reminds me that getting input is worth the effort.

When it comes to making decisions and avoiding overcommitment and burnout, we must learn from our mistakes. But we don't just learn that we have to be able to say no and we have to have a good methodology for arriving at no. We learn to trust other people when they speak into our lives. We learn to let people into our lives in a way that allows them to speak.

We are not islands—none of us are. But neither are any of us immune from thinking that we have all the answers or that no one understands what we are going through. It's true that God gives us a free will. If he doesn't force us to do something, then no one else should either. God guides us through prayer and through virtues such as wisdom, but he also gives us friends and mentors who can see our situation more clearly and somehow remember things about us that we forget.

Build those kinds of relationships and get feedback. You aren't asking other people to make decisions for you. You're asking for their point of view.

This works in big decisions and small ones. There have been many times that I've texted or called a friend to hash out feelings of fatigue or sadness, only to discover, through their feedback, that I was not seeing these issues clearly.

Life is an adventure. Maybe that's our takeaway here. Even if we work hard and come up with the right formula and do the right things for the right reasons, we will still, on occasion, experience feelings of fatigue and burnout.

It's okay. It's a side effect of being human.

Find Joy (and Help) in the Adventure

Sometimes life is just crazy because it has to be.

I was looking through an old journal recently—one from the end of a school year in which we had a lot going on. May isn't for wimps, by the way, but that's another story for another time.

At that time, according to the journal, I somehow ended up being in charge of the awards banquet at our school, which includes a catered dinner in our gymnasium. This event is generally spearheaded by a parent of a rising senior, and because there were only ten students in my son's class, it fell to me. All the other parents had major life stuff going on, and I was in a position to be in charge peacefully.

Months earlier I had offered to be in charge of the reception that would take place right after the graduation ceremony. Graduation takes place a few days after the awards banquet, and I figured, when I said yes to doing the awards banquet, it was really just a matter of buying a few more balloons and such when I went shopping.

Around that same time, I also started helping plan a big shindig for our high school principal who was retiring after being a founding member of our school thirty years prior. I was not in charge of everything, but I handled several aspects of the party.

So there, in my notebook of information, I had a page for each of these events. A list of things to do, things to buy, and things to accomplish for each event. It sounds overwhelming—the very definition of overcommitment—and at moments it felt that way.

But here's why I said yes to all of it. One, I knew I was the person in the position to get the job done. Several of the other moms and dads were going through hard times with aging parents and other issues. I was happy to be able to help.

Two, each of these endeavors came with a helper, the perfect person in every case. A word of advice: having a helper should be nonnegotiable when you sign up for a big task. I said a prayer that God would show me the best person to help, and he did. In each case, the person who stepped in to manage aspects of the events or to help me with decisions was capable, generous, and got the job done.

You can do a lot, but you shouldn't do it alone.

By the end of those intense weeks of planning and executing and celebrating all that goodness, I was tired. But I was also relieved and felt a lot of joy. I had pushed myself, because I knew I could. It was short-term and it was tough, but it was also very rewarding. I hadn't quite overcommitted—I had people who threw themselves into the work so that it was all manageable.

Don't go it alone. We're all in this together, and it's a joy to be part of the adventure!

As a body is one though it has many parts, and all the parts of the body, though many, are one body, so also Christ. . . .

Now the body is not a single part, but many. . . . If [one] part suffers, all the parts suffer with it; if one part is honored, all the parts share its joy.

Now you are Christ's body, and individually parts of it. (1 Corinthians 12:12, 14, 26-27)

Do your best, and God will take care of the rest.

Prayer Starter

Serenity Prayer

O God, grant me the serenity to accept the things I cannot change the courage to change the things I can and the wisdom to know the difference.

Living one day at a time, enjoying one moment at a time. Accepting hardships as the pathway to peace. Taking, as he did, the sinful world as it is, not as I would have it. Trusting that he will make all things right if I surrender to His will; that I may be reasonably happy in this life, and supremely happy with Him forever.[24]

Notes

1. Greg McKeown, *Essentialism: The Disciplined Pursuit of Less* (New York, NY: Crown Publishing Group, 2014), 4.

2. McKeown, 4.

3. St. Teresa of of Ávila (1515-1582), https://www.goodreads.com/quotes/66880-christ-has-no-body-now-but-yours-no-hands-no.

4. Charles de Foucauld (1858-1916), Prayer of Abandonment, https://www.ewtn.com/catholicism/devotions/prayer-ofabandonment-361.

5. Pope St. John Paul II, *Dover Beach*, "It Is Jesus That You Seek When You Dream of Happiness," September 25, 2016, https://lifeondoverbeach.wordpress.com/2016/09/25/john-paul-ii-it-is-jesus-that-you-seek-when-you-dream-of-happiness/.

6. Henri J. M. Nouwen, *Discernment: Reading the Signs of Daily Life* (New York, NY: HarperCollins Publishers, 2013), 3.

7. *Discernment*, 5.

8. Bishop Robert Barron, October 18, 2019, https://www.facebook.com/BishopRobertBarron/posts/2548188165220295.

9. Isaiah 26:20

10. Proverbs 4:23

11. Isaiah 45:3

12. 1 Corinthians 13:10

13. St. John of the Cross, *A Spiritual Canticle of the Soul and the Bridegroom Christ* (Grand Rapids, MI: Christian Classics Ethereal Library, 2000), Stanza 1:12, http://www.documentacatholicaomnia.eu/03d/1542-1591,_Ioannes_a_Cruce,_A_Spiritual_Canticle_Of_The_Soul,_EN.pdf.

14. Sr. Faustina Maria Pia, SV, Litany of Trust, https://sistersoflife.org/wp-content/uploads/2019/07/Mobile-Litany-of-Trust.pdf.

15. Henry J. M. Nouwen, *With Open Hands* (South Bend, IN: Ave Maria Press, 1972).

16. *With Open Hands*, 20.

17. *With Open Hands*, 20.

18. Cardinal Merry del Val, *The Prayer Book for Jesuits*, 1963, Litany of Humility, https://www.ewtn.com/catholicism/devotions/litany-of-humility-245.

19. *Catechism,* footnote 121, Genesis 2:2.

20. *Catechism,* footnote 122, cf. *Gaudium et Spes*, Section 3.

21. Donna-Marie Cooper O'Boyle, ed., *By Dawn's Early Light: Prayers and Meditations for Catholic Military Wives* (Manchester, NH: Sophia Institute Press, 2017), 33.

22. Pope St. John Paul II, *Zenit*, October 22, 2018, "Saint John Paul II: 'Be Not Afraid,'" https://zenit.org/articles/saint-john-paul-ii-be-not-afraid/.

23. Loyola Press, "Prayer to the Holy Spirit," https://www.loyolapress.com/our-catholic-faith/prayer/traditional-catholic-prayers/prayers-every-catholic-should-know/prayer-to-the-holy-spirit.

24. Catholic Online, "Serenity Prayer," https://www.catholic.org/prayers/prayer.